AN IMMIGRANT, A HOMESTEADER, AND SHEEP

AN IMMIGRANT, A HOMESTEADER, AND SHEEP

GRACE E LARSON

An Immigrant, a Homesteader, and Sheep

Copyright © 2021 by Grace E Larson. All rights reserved.

No part of this publication may be reproduced, stored in a retrieval system or transmitted in any way by any means, electronic, mechanical, photocopy, recording or otherwise without the prior permission of the author except as provided by USA copyright law.

The opinions expressed by the author are not necessarily those of URLink Print and Media.

1603 Capitol Ave., Suite 310 Cheyenne, Wyoming USA 82001
1-888-980-6523 | admin@urlinkpublishing.com

URLink Print and Media is committed to excellence in the publishing industry.

Book design copyright © 2021 by URLink Print and Media. All rights reserved.

Published in the United States of America

Library of Congress Control Number: 2020925451
ISBN 978-1-64753-614-5 (Paperback)
ISBN 978-1-64753-615-2 (Hardback)
ISBN 978-1-64753-616-9 (Digital)

27.08.21

Contents

Acknowledgements..9
Introduction..11
Dan Poloson..13
Military Draft Card...15
1920 United States Federal Census....................................17
Learning To Pack, Speak English, And Getting Married..............20
Mae's Death Dan's Trips To Romania 22
Grace Remembers Dan And Mae.......................................24
1930 United States Federal Census....................................26
Mae Poloson..29
Mae Arrives In Logan..30
Mae Homesteads..33
Mae Builds And Plants..37
Mae's Certificate Of Homestead...39
Mae's Mother: Mary E. Deschamps Certificate Of Homestead.....40
Mae Poloson Homestead Crops And Home 41
More Sheep Ranchers..47
Marie's Memories Marie: Wolf Creek 69
Going To Sheep Camp..72
We Move To Rattlesnake Gulch 73
Jim And Klonda Howser 74
Homesteads, Chores, And School......................................76
Rattlesnakes And Our Garden..79
Hay And Cold Winters 80
Cooking And Cooks..83
Lambing And Shearing..85
Mamaliga 86
The Depression 88
Nick And Anna Lascu 92
Sheep Men And Rustlers 95

Bert And Fay: Herron Ranch	97
Cowboying, Gardening,. And School	98
Wrecks	100
Water, Hired Men, And Electricity	101
Trip To Browning–Area Sheep Ranchers	103
Trailing Sheep And Hunting Bear	105
Lost With Lost Sheep	108
Mutton, Messy Street, And The Law	110
The Real Work Begins	111
Fred And I After Ranch Life	113
Ernestine Marie Poloson	117
Fred Harris Poloson	133
Fay's Story	154
Wild Horse Island Roundup	171
Albert Raymond Poloson	182
Mae Poloson Poems Retyped By Jeanne Poloson Bronec	205
Coyote's Serenade	207
Moonstruck	208
When October Turns The Maple Leaves To Gold	209
Sunset Light	211
I Believe	213
Compensation	214
This 'N' That	215
Campfire Reverie	216
Prairies At Midnight	217
By Mae Poloson	218
By May Poloson	219
Kiss It And Make It Well	220
"Mother Knows Best"	221
"Isolationist"	222
"To Kathie"	223
Lost Faith	224
Dry Lander	225
Little Joys	226
I Tried Anyway	227
Big Butch, Little Butch	228

Spring Time	230
Waiting For A Letter	231
Don't' Think You're The Whole Corn Field	232
When Golden Autumn Leaves Are Drifting Down	233
Odds & Ends	234
Tuffy	235
Starlight, Star Bright	236
Unfinished Echoes	237
(I Believe)	238
To A Sparrow	239
Come Back Elaine	240
Envy	241
Shadows	242
Christmas Eve In Rattlesnake Gulch	244
Broken Toys	245
Just Because I Love You	247
Brief Return	248
Blue Eyes From Texas	249
Each Heart Knoweth Its Own Bitterness	252
God Of The Nation	255
Odds And Ends	256
Tears And Beer (To' 'Old Fritz)	257
Honey Chile	259
"Sure That's Different"	260
Splash	262
Valentine	263
Dreams	264
If I Had Wings	265
Beloved	267
Hickory Whistle	268
Moonstruck	270
Coyote	272
Indian Summer Waltz	274
Song Of The Unknown Road	275
Riding Thru The Silver Sage With You	277
The Little Black Dog	278

Shining Star..*280*
Homesick *281*
Trees And Water *282*
Signs Of Spring...*283*
Beanery Babe's Busted Romance.................................*284*
First Rattler *285*
To Rattlesnake From Rattlebrain *286*
Riding Up To Grapevine Hollow *287*
Black Duck..*288*
Gray Wolf's Dance...*289*
Rural Romance..*290*
Little New House *291*
Circumstantial Evidence..*292*
Legend Of The War Dragon *293*
Epilogue...295

ACKNOWLEDGEMENTS

Department Of Interior Homestead Records

Ancestry.com

Marie Poloson Tapes And Photos

Bert Poloson Tapes And Photos

Fred Poloson Photos

Fay Poloson Haynes Photos, Memories, and Writings

Rosie Swisher King Memories

Mae Poloson Poems

Biography Information From Settlers and Sodbusters

Valley Press (Ronan, Montana)

Hungry Horse News (Kalispell, Montana)

AQHA Journal

Western Horseman

INTRODUCTION

Dan & Mae DeSchamps Poloson Family History–A Story Of Faith & Courage By Grace Larson Based on Memories from Marie, Bert, and Fay.

"Cherish All Of Your Memories For They Are The Bricks & Mortar Of Who You Are".

This thought brought to mind what Ada Gould, a long time family friend, had said one day, "You come from good stock." She was referring to my grandparents and their children, Marie (my mother), Fred, Fay, and Bert.

This story is dedicated to my grandparents for their courage and foresight. Because of this I have been blessed with life and liberty in this great country.

Dan Poloson was born in Porumbac, Romania October 26, 1895. He came to America at the age of 20 in 1916. Mae DeSchamps Poloson was born in Indian Territory near Mansfield, Arkansas February 8, 1889. When she was 21 she traveled west by train from Arkansas to Three Forks, MT.

Dan came to this country for the freedom to work hard and build a good life for himself and his family. Mae's forefathers came to America from Scotland, Ireland, and France for freedom from religious persecution and government control. This was especially horrible for the DeSchamps before and after the French Revolution; that was when the Huguenots were jailed, tortured, and killed.

America, where the "Declaration Of Independence" declared: "We hold these truths to be self evident, that all men are created equal; that they are endowed by their Creator with certain unalienable rights; that among these are life, liberty, and the pursuit of happiness." The Constitution states that "Congress shall make no law respecting an establishment of religion, or prohibiting the free exercise thereof."

This wonderful country and its freedoms gave my grandparents the opportunities many never get to experience. Grandpa and Grandma knew how to work hard and they were able to overcome hardships along the way. They passed those qualities on to their children and grandchildren.

Remember we come from "Good Stock."

Caption: Mae and Dan

DAN POLOSON

Dan Poloson was born in Porumbac, Romania October 26, 1895. His parents, Nick and Lina Copotina Poloson raised sheep; Dan learned to herd and care for sheep at an early age. The people of this small village were very poor; photos taken over sixty years after Dan left his family and village show ox carts on the unpaved streets and few homes with running water or bathroom facilities. The architecture is the same. The photo below of Dan at a wedding in Romania shows their dress to be very close to what it was near the turn of the twentieth century. This was taken on one of Dan's trips back to Romania. Dan is third from the left.

Dan left Romania in 1916 when he was twenty years old. He and a friend decided they didn't want to spend their lives working in a factory in Romania. Dan was sea sick from the time he left Romania until the ship came to the shore of America. The trip took twenty four days. His first stop was in Kokomo, Indiana then on to Chicago, Illinois where he worked in a packing plant. Working conditions were horrible but a job was imperative since he was flat broke. His friend found a job milking cows but Dan's thoughts were the thousands of sheep he'd heard about at Helena, Montana. Helena was headquarters for many Romanian sheep herders. Dan landed at the Bristol Hotel which was operated by a Romanian named Bozdock. From there he went to work for Sieben and Grimes, a large sheep ranch near Wolf Creek.

The Montana Central Railroad wound through the valley near the Sieben Ranch holdings of 115,000 acres. Supplies were brought in by rail. Henry Sieben had purchased the ranch in 1897. Dan worked for Henry Sieben for four years.

MILITARY DRAFT CARD

Dan had to sign up for the Military Draft in June of 1917. His occupation was in agriculture so that may be why he wasn't drafted. His card below:

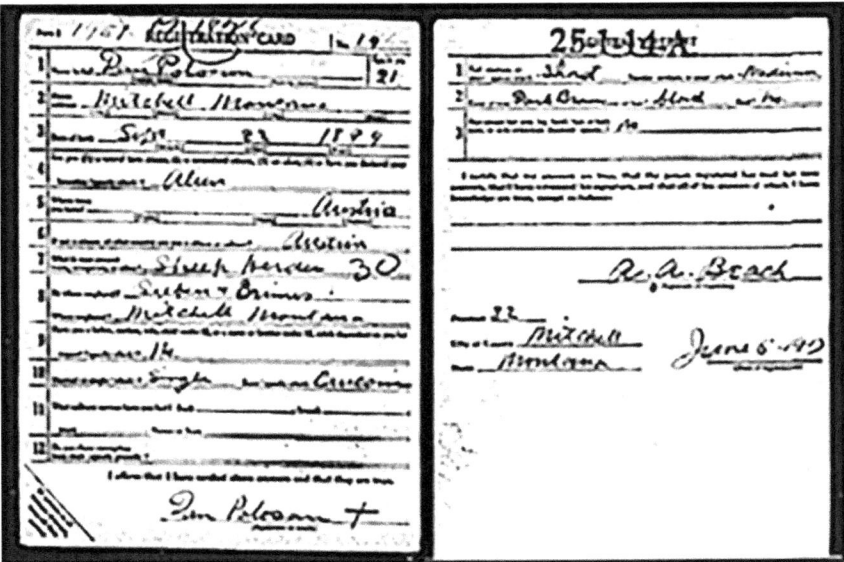

World War I Draft Registration Card
Name:Dan Polosom
County:Lewis and Clark State:Montana
Birth Date:22 Sep 1894
Race:Caucasian)
FHL Roll Number:1711434

It is unknown why Dan put Austria as his country of origin and his birth date as September 22, 1894. He arrived in the United States in 1916 just before Romania was pulled into WW I. It is possible he had a safety reason for this. Our own country under President Wilson was very suspicious of citizens and immigrants. So that may be the reason. Whatever it was, Dan must have had assistance in filling this out and this person must have been protecting him. Dan signed with an X so the person helping him signed his name. Dan was very limited in English as he'd only been in this country about a year.

1920 UNITED STATES FEDERAL CENSUS

Dan went to work on the Herrin sheep ranch in 1920 staying there until he and Mae bought the ranch near Lonepine, Montana in 1929.

Name: Dan Poloson
Home In 1920: Cartersville, Lewis and Clark County, Montana
Age: 25
Est. Birth Year: About 1895
Birthplace: Romania
Relation To Head Of House: Hired Man
Father's Birth Place: Romania
Mother's Birth Place: Romania
Marital Status: Single
Race: White
Sex: Male
Year Of Immigration: 1916
Able To Read: Yes
Able To Write: Yes
Neighbors: None Listed

Household Members:
Harland J. Herrin Ranch Owner Age 54
Mary E. Herrin Wife Of Owner Age 39
Mabel A. O Connell Sister-in-law of Herrins Age 20
John O Connell Brother-in-law of Herrins Age 28
John Taylor Born in Scotland 1877 Age 43
Won Young (woman) Born in China 1868 Age 52
Dan Poloson Age 25
Amos P. Chase Born in Maine 1850 Age 70
Alice Bloyer (man) Born in Romania 1880 Age 40
Immigrated to America 1904 or 1907
Elie Cadacareo (man) Born in Romania 1879 Age 41
Immigrated to America 1913

Caption: Dan & Prince Herrin Ranch

Caption: Dan & his Sheep Oct. 1960

Caption: Poloson Sheep Late 1930's

Caption: Pack String At Fishtrap 1950's

LEARNING TO PACK, SPEAK ENGLISH, AND GETTING MARRIED

Having never been around horses, Dan didn't know how to put a halter on or load a pack horse; his packs would fall off. With the help of another herder and lots of practice he became an excellent horseman and packer. He could easily move and set up sheep camps. His work with sheep was near the ranch in the winter but summers found him in steep and beautiful mountain country. This mountain experience was very beneficial when he leased summer pasture from the Forest Service in the Cabinet Mountains, and later the St. Joe area of the Idaho mountains.

Dan could neither write or speak English when he migrated to the United States. He was Naturalized September 23, 1928 while he was still in the employ of Mr. Herrin. His acceptance as a Naturalized Citizen was because of good references, hard work, and not because he could read a word of the questions that were to be answered.

The Herrins were very good to Dan. After Dan & Mae were married they lived in a house on the ranch east of Helena near present day Wolf Creek. Harland Herrin was listed in the 1880 United States Census as being 17 years of age and residing in Jefferson County, Montana. He became known as a very prominent Montana businessman.

Dan and Mae were married in Helena, Montana on March 4, 1922. How they met is unknown. Mae might have been teaching area immigrants how to speak English.

Their children were born in Helena; Ernestine Marie, March 3, 1923: Fred Harris, March 31, 1924: Fay Elinore, January 4, 1926: Albert Raymond, September 6, 1927.

Eighteen years after Dan's arrival in America he had enough money set aside to buy the ranch near Lonepine, Montana just before the great depression of 1929. They made a go of it on the ranch even though times were hard and money was scarce. Dan and Mae were able to build the ranch into one of the finest in the area through hard work, perseverance, and honesty.

Dan, from a poor village in Romania, and Mae from a family thrown into poverty when her father died. Mae was five hears old when her mother was left alone with eight children and a younger brother to raise.

Dan was generous to a fault. He helped the Indian families that camped by the upper spring; the women would walk down to the cook house where they were given food to take back to camp. Bert would walk up to visit them; he was young and really impressed the Indian people. They wanted to adopt the Poloson children into the Flathead tribe. Many of the Indians worked for Dan & Mae at the ranch during lambing and shearing. Dan had several Indian herders in the mountains. He also helped many of the small ranchers and farmers in the area.

MAE'S DEATH DAN'S TRIPS TO ROMANIA

*Photo of Magdalena and Aurelia
Poloson Ranch 1974*

Poloson Ranch

Mae passed away in 1967; after her passing Dan began planning a trip to Romania. He had sold the sheep and his cattle needed less care. He delighted in helping his sister, Magdalena, when he traveled to Romania. He rented an apartment for her making sure it had a water heater, stove, and comfortable furnishings. Then he bought a car for her; Magdalena couldn't drive but a nephew could.

Dan brought Magdalena and her daughter, Aurelia, to the ranch for a month long visit in 1974. They got to see the Poloson Ranch and much of western Montana, and they were able to meet Dan's family.

GRACE REMEMBERS DAN AND MAE

Dan (Grandpa) was a patient man; he had to be to work with sheep. He wasn't one to gossip; I recall a neighbor who had been giving Dan all the news. When she left his comment was, "she knows too much." I remember how hard he worked especially during lambing. Dan would go for hours without sleep napping in his chair for an hour or so then back to the lambing shed.

My memories of Mae (Grandma) are of her reading every chance she got. Her table had many magazines that I loved to look through. She could cook the best eggs; mine had to be broken because the yolk had to be well done. She had Ritz and Cheezit crackers for my sister, Alice, & I to snack on. And she had planted a peach pit that grew into a producing tree. It had several big, luscious peaches but they were saved for Grandpa. I'm sure they weren't near as big as they seemed then.

Dan Packing Out A Deer

1930 UNITED STATES FEDERAL CENSUS

Name: Dan Poloson
Age: 37
Home in 1930: Polson, Lake County, Montana
Estimated birth year: abt 1895
Birthplace: Romania
Relation to Head of House: Head
Spouse's name: Mae Poloson
Race: White
Household Members:
Dan Poloson 37
Mae Poloson 43
Fred Poloson 6
Marie Poloson 7
Fay Poloson 4
Albert R Poloson 2
Fred Harris 56

The Poloson Ranch was located between Lonepine and Niarada, Montana. Most of the ranch land was in Lake County, county seat in Polson, and some was in Sanders County, county seat Thompson Falls. The ranch was a winter home for the sheep. They were in the mountains from late May through September. The ranch was dry grass land with very good springs and lots of sage brush.

An Immigrant, a Homesteader, and Sheep

Dan Poloson & The Grizzly Bear

Ann (Mrs. Fred) Poloson on left
Dan Poloson early 1960's

MAE POLOSON

Mae was born in what was then Indian Territory near Mansfield, Arkansas February 8, 1889 to Sinkler Capers and Mary Holleman DeSchamps. Mae was one of ten children: Mollie (1877), Samuel (1878), John (1879), Louis (1883), Minnie (1884), Mae, Maude (1891), Jessie (1893), and James and Capers who died as infants. Mae's father was a blacksmith and Baptist minister.

In 1894 Sinkler Capers DeSchamps died leaving Mae's mother to care for the family and her younger brother, Logan (1884), alone. Mae was 5 and Samuel, the oldest, was 16. Mae said the family took in laundry and they all did whatever work could be found.

Eventually, 2 of Mae's brothers found jobs on the railroad. They became familiar with the west and the new Homestead Act of 1909. Hoping for a better life, Mae, her sister Maude, and brother Louis left Arkansas by train arriving in Pocatello, Idaho, in 1910. The photo below was taken after they arrived in Pocatello.

Left to right: Maude, Louis, and Mae.

MAE ARRIVES IN LOGAN

Mae, Maude, and Louis traveled on to the Logan & Three Forks areas of Montana. Mae found employment cooking for train crews and passengers at the Northern Pacific Railroad roundhouse in Logan. Logan's 1910 population was 200 with most working for the railroad or mining. Other businesses were the livery stable, 5 taverns, a barbershop (haircuts were 35 cents, a shave 15 cents), a restaurant run by a Chinaman, several mercantiles, and a house of ill repute down by the river. Bums and professional hobos were always in Logan coming in or leaving on one of the trains. Logan was a "melting pot "with English, Irish, Italian, Greeks, Germans, Austrians, Poles, Chinese, French, and a few Negroes. During the summer it was not uncommon for a band of Indians to camp close by. They were very poor so lived by begging, stealing, or butchering cows killed by trains. They also traded artistic goods they made. Some items were made from the bones of buffalo. Buffalo bones were scattered all over the Gallatin and Madison Valley; some of the heads still had horns attached.

Logan Roundhouse & Sand House

Riders In Front Of the Round House

Logan was two blocks long and every building faced the tracks

Logan Late 1880's Cabin Built In 1863 Still Occupied In 1970

Louis had worked for the railroad in Arkansas and was a member of the Brotherhood Of Railroad Engineers & Firemen, so he went to work for the Northern Pacific. Maude took house keeping jobs and finally found work at the Sacajawea Hotel in Three Forks. Mae went to work as a cook and waitress at the Sacajawea since Three Forks was closer to her homestead. The Chicago, Milwaukee, and St Paul Railway brought a boom to the area. The hotel was a busy place with railroad crews and passengers arriving for meals and lodging. The hotel has been refurbished and continues to serve guests in 2011.

MAE HOMESTEADS

Mae filed for a homestead August 18, 1910. Louis filed on land that bordered Mae's. Maude at 19 wasn't old enough so she helped Mae and Louis prove theirs. Their mother, Mary Emaline, arrived in Montana in 1911. She filed for a homestead that bordered Mae & Louis on June 27, 1914.

She worked her homestead during the crop growing seasons and worked away from home, mainly in Three Forks, the rest of the year. Homesteaders had to request permission to be away from their land and notify the land office of their return. They were allowed five months absence a year.

Water was hauled in by wagon from the Missouri River near Tosten, Montana. Hoes, rakes, and shovels were the garden tools of that era. Homesteaders could hire a neighbor with a team to plow and harrow the garden. Mae raked the sod, picked rock, and planted seeds. She planted a 5 acre garden! Some years she expanded to wheat or oats along with the garden.

Mae did most of her business in Radersburg because it was closer to her homestead than Three Forks. In the early 1900's travel by wagon or horseback was across country via the shortest route. Highway 287 wasn't even a thought then nor was the road which goes out to where Mae's homestead was located.

Mae's poem sums up life on the frontier:

> The poets sing of birds in spring,
> and silver streams and lakes
> Could they but stand on this dry land
> they'd sing of rattlesnakes.

Photos of Radersburg Buildings Taken In 2010

There are three deer in this photo

Radersburg Baptist Church

MAE BUILDS AND PLANTS

Mae's home was finished January of 1911. She moved onto the homestead February 1, 1911. Mae was given full title to the land September 30, 1916. She had to list the crops by the year planted when she applied for title:

1912: Broke 2 acres and planted garden vegetables. (breaking most likely hired)

1913: Broke 3 acres and planted garden vegetables. (cost about $6.50 an acre)

1914: Replowed 3 acres and planted garden vegetables. (plowing likely hired)

1915: Broke 10 acres and planted 1 acre to garden vegetables, 5 acres to wheat, and 4 acres to oats. Broke 20 acres. (surely hired)

1916: Planted about a half acre to garden, 12 acres to oats, and the balance of the 35 acres to wheat. Thrashed about 100 bushels of oats and 100 bushels of wheat. (I'm sure hired except for her garden)

Mae listed her house as Frame House 9 x 12.
She had built 2 miles of 3 wire fence.
Total value of improvements: $250.

Mae sold a right of way through her homestead to the Radersburg Railroad Company. The right of way took about 2 acres but they never used it. I don't know who Mae sold her land to when she moved to Helena. This would have been in 1918 or 1919. She cooked at the Florence Crittenton Home for girls, and the Montana Deaconess School for orphans.

Charles N. Crittenton began one of the greatest philanthropic movements of all time when he established the Florence Crittenton Homes. On April 19, 1883 the first home opened its doors in New

York City. This was the first philanthropic organization ever chartered by a special act of congress. The Helena home was incorporated June 12, 1900. The home was licensed by the State Of Montana.

Montana Deaconess School was incorporated under the laws of Montana in 1909. It is under the auspices of the Methodist Church and operated by Methodist Deaconesses. In 1954 the name changed to Inter-Mountain Deaconess Home for Children, and in 1989 the name changed to Intermountain Children's Home. I don't know if Mae continued to work for a while after she & Dan were married, or if she moved to the Herrin Ranch right away.

MAE'S CERTIFICATE OF HOMESTEAD

Department of the Interior

United States Land Office

Serial No. 9435
Receipt No.

Certificate.
Homestead

It is hereby certified that, pursuant to the provisions of Section 2291, Revised Statutes of the United States, Annie V. De Schweng, of Three Forks, Mont.,

has made payment in full for

Section 4
Township 1 North, Range 1 East, M.P., Meridian,
containing 160 acres.

Now, therefore, be it known that, on presentation of this Certificate to the COMMISSIONER OF THE GENERAL LAND OFFICE, the said Annie V. De Schweng

shall be entitled to receive a Patent for the land above described, if all things be found regular.

Register

PAT NO 547740
OCT 17 1916

APPROVED SEP 30 1916

Division R.

MAE'S MOTHER: MARY E. DESCHAMPS CERTIFICATE OF HOMESTEAD

O.H.B.

Serial No. 09473
Receipt No. 1440021-2021805

Final Certificate.
Homestead.

Proof made under Act June 6, 1912.

September 1, 1917.

It is hereby certified that, pursuant to the provisions of Section 2291, Revised Statutes of the United States, Mary E. DeSchamps, Three Forks, Montana, has made payment in full for

Lot 3, SE 1/4, NE 1/4, E 1/2 SE 1/4 Section 3 Township 2 North, Range 1 East, M.M. Meridian, containing 162.10 acres.

Now, therefore, be it known that, on presentation of this Certificate to the COMMISSIONER OF THE GENERAL LAND OFFICE, the said Mary E. DeSchamps shall be entitled to receive a Patent for the land above described if all then be found regular.

_____, Register.

NOTE—A duplicate of this Certificate is issued to the claimant as notice of the acceptance of the proof and payment, and of the allowance of the entry by the Register and Receiver.
The original is forwarded to the General Land Office, with the entry papers, for approval by the Commissioner of the General Land Office and issuance of patent.
The duplicate copy forwarded to the claimant should be held until notice of issuance of patent is received.
In all correspondence concerning the entry in connection with which this Certificate is issued, refer to the NAME OF THE LAND OFFICE and the SERIAL NUMBER noted hereon.

Posted Oct-22 in Vol 21, p. 25, by R.J.R., Div. "O."
APPROVED March 29, 1918
By C. M. Archibald, Division C

PAT NO 634605 June 12, 1918

MAE POLOSON HOMESTEAD CROPS AND HOME

Before I continue with Dan and Mae's history I want to record some of the history of the area sheep ranchers; the most notable were the Lascus. Many of these ranchers will be mentioned by Marie (Mom) and Bert (my uncle) in their memories recorded on tape in 2008 and 2010. Marie passed away December 20, 2008. Thankfully she spent the winter of 2007/2008 with us and I was able to record some of her memories.

In April of 2010 we took a trip to Bert and Grace Poloson's near Polson, Montana. Bert and Grace had been making notes from memories of the sheep ranchers, herders, and hay suppliers that lived in Sanders and Lake county. I was able to record a lot of those memories.

Bert spent many months in the mountains with his father, Dan. Fay Poloson Haynes (my aunt) shared memories of the Poloson Ranch and her trip to Romania with Dan (her father). Bill Haynes' (Fay's husband) name will come up in these recorded memories.

Fred Poloson (my uncle) passed away February 18, 2006. Fred also spent a lot of time in the mountains with Dan. Photos and recollections from Marie and Bert have memories of Fred and his wife, Ann.

Rosie Swisher King has been helpful with her memories of the Lascus, the Polosons, the Swishers, and others in the Lonepine / Hot Springs valley.

Ancestry.com provided many of the census, marriage, birth, death, military, and immigration records.

Lonepine Murray Memorial Cemetery is home to many of those mentioned in this history.

Both Lascus were Romanians and were Dan & Mae's closest neighbors. This was the world's second largest sheep barn pictured below in the late 1930's. It was five hundred feet long and one hundred twenty feet wide. Nick had this built in the mid-twenties.

Nick & Anna Lascu sheep shed

Emery Swisher and Alan Voorhies cut and hauled poles for the shed.

There were one hundred kerosene lanterns in the sheep shed. During lambing one man was hired to take care of these lanterns. The glass would get smoked up and had to be cleaned; the lanterns also required frequent filling.

Nick had three thousand sheep. When Lambing and shearing were finished the sheep were trailed to Marion, Montana where they were loaded onto railroad cars and shipped to Browning for summer pasture. Bert went with Nick a few times. Nick's range was near Duck Lake on the Blackfoot Indian Reservation. My father, Tim Baker, went with Nick a few times trailing then herding once they reached the reservation.

Tom King and Arvid Kopp worked for Nick for several years during lambing. Whenever they'd meet in later years Arvid would say to Tom, "Time to water them sheep boys. "Arvid was born November 4, 1915 and passed away January 13, 1992. He lived and died in Sanders County, Montana. Tom King was born December 2, 1911 and passed away May 4, 1980. He also lived and died in Sanders

County. Rosie Swisher and Tom King were married August 16, 1947. Marie (Mom) and Rosie attended Lonepine school together.

Steve Vulles worked for Nick when he was in high school. He graduated from the Lonepine School with Fred. Nick bought hay from area farmers including the Swishers. Anna Lascu always timed her arrival with Rosie Swisher King's birth in May of 1925. Nick and Anna never had children. Their close neighbors, Dan & Mae, had four; the Swishers had five and all were close to the same age.

Nick and Anna were also good hearted. When Emery Swisher was hospitalized at Ft. Harrison they bought eggs from his wife, Myrtle Mae. Nick handed her a five dollar bill for fifteen dozen eggs; that was a lot of money then. Rosie said that bill seemed huge to her as she'd never seen money like that. She saw her first one hundred dollar bill in the early 1980's when her son came home from working in the oil fields. He was paying for goods with one hundred dollar bills.

Marie (Mom) worked for Nick and Anna; Marie's employment continued after she and my father were divorced in 1941. Charlie Hurst was the bus driver then.

The 1920 United States Census:

Emery Swisher Age 33
Single The 1930 Census:
Emery H. Swisher Age 43
Married Myrtle M. Swisher Age 22
Children:
Rosie M. Swisher Age 4 Ruth M. Swisher Age 2
Lyle, Joan, and Murel were born later and not listed on the 1930 census.

Myrtle Swisher passed away March 31, 1992. She was 85 years old having been born May 21, 1907. Emery Swisher passed away November 23, 1967.

He was 80 years old; birth was March 4, 1887. Emery served in World War I.

The 1920 United States Census:

Nick Lascu
Age 34
Home was Moise, Montana Birthplace Romania 1886 Year of Immigration was 1910.
The 1930 Census gave his home as Sanders County, Montana.
Nicolae Lascu passed away June 23, 1956 at 72 years.
Anna Lascu was born in 1908 and passed away March 31, 1966 at 72 years.

Alice remembers the Lascu's home with its beautiful bedrooms, colorful quilts, and pretty dolls displayed on the beds. She also recalls Grandpa Dan telling her about the time Anna was coming out of the Safeway store when the ties on her panties came loose. It was war time and elastic was scarce so panties were held on by strings that tied. He said she just stepped out of her panties, picked them up, put them in her purse, and said, "Me pay for 'em me keep 'em" and walked on down the street.

Marie Poloson
Lascu Place
1939

Mom at Lascu's 1940

Mom & Myrtle Hayworth

MORE SHEEP RANCHERS

BERT:
The Polson Sheep Company, owned by a man named Fairchild, was very active during the early 1940's. They had four to five thousand head of sheep and were the largest sheep outfit in the area. Their headquarters were located on Irvin Flats which is located in the northwest corner of the Flathead Indian Reservation.

Louis B. Matt (Bud) had several hundred head of sheep. His place was located on the reservation not to far from the Buffalo Bridge which crosses the Flathead River. Bud's lease was above the Pablo Ranch in the Big Draw, and he also had a lease above the Poloson Ranch. Bud Matt was a Flathead Indian tribal member. He was born February 6, 1912 and passed away July 21, 1989.

Roy Atkinson's band of sheep numbered around one thousand. His place was near Charlo, Montana which is located near the center of the Flathead Reservation. Mr. Atkinson was born September 13, 1887 and passed away May 15, 1974.

Wayne Schmmal had around a thousand head of sheep. His place was located between Dixon and Perma on the reservation. Mr. Schmmal moved his sheep through the Poloson Ranch when they were trailed to summer pasture.

Harry Burgess had a small band of two–three hundred head. His place was located between Perma and Paradise, Montana. Dan Poloson took Mr. Burgess and other small sheep rancher's wool to sell with his own. Harry Burgess, a World War I veteran, was born May 20, 1887. I wasn't able to locate his date of death.

Ira Baxter's sheep ranch was located north of Hot Springs. He had around a hundred head and shipped his wool with Dan Poloson's. Ira Baxter was born November 15, 1906 and passed away in July of 1982.

Warren McClum had between five hundred and a thousand head at his place west of Niarada. He trailed his sheep to the Rogers Lake country near Marion, Montana for summer pasture. From what I could find Mr. McClum may have been of Indian ancestry. He was born December 29, 1885. I couldn't find a death date.

Paul Worth had a hundred head on his place northwest of Niarada. His place was located on the edge of the reservation. Mr. Worth was born February 28, 1886 and passed away in September of 1966.

Howard Nye's ranch was located near the Big Bend of the Flathead River on the Flathead Indian Reservation. He had around a thousand head and had enough pasture on his place. Mr. Nye was a World War I veteran born in 1890. He passed away March 2, 1972.

Howard Burton's place was located on Irvin Flats. He had several hundred head of sheep and pastured them on his place. Mr. Burton was born in 1912 and passed away August 22, 1978.

Bert and Tuffy on the Carlin house steps

An Immigrant, a Homesteader, and Sheep

Anna Lascu and Mrs. Roger Rosette

Charles Spear Bracket had a couple hundred head on his ranch north of Plains, Montana. He had enough pasture for his herd. Mr. Bracket was born February 27, 1923 and passed away February 6, 2010.

Cecil and Pearl (a guy) Argo ran six or seven hundred head on their ranch which was located on Camas Prairie, south of Hot Springs, Montana. Cecil Argo was born in 1891 and passed away March 9, 1963. Pearl Argo was born in 1881 and passed away March 29, 1958.

Bert Young had about one hundred head of sheep on his place near the Little Thompson River and the Cabinet Mountains. His place was a stop for the Poloson sheep and herders along their way to summer pasture, and on their way back to the ranch in the Fall.

Dan Poloson had the last sheep ranch of any size when he retired in 1963. By 1976 the area had about 425 ewes with most belonging to the Jolma, Heidegger, and McCallum ranches. This is from an article in the Daily Missoulian by Judy Dorsey. She noted that sheep ranching was still profitable even though herds had never been smaller. Coyotes were eating up the profits on the Brown Ranch near Niarada so in 1975 they decided to sell their sheep. Paul Heidinger was losing two lambs a week; he had 350 ewes and was down to 60 with plans to get out of the sheep business until he could build corrals to protect the sheep from coyotes. When Verdie McCallum heard that the Jolmas' were lambing out 171 yearling ewes she said she was going to light two candles for them.

Dan and Mae's sheep ranch began when they bought 1700 acres and a herd of sheep from Michael Quilligan in 1928. Mr. Quilligan was retiring; he was seventy three having been born in 1855. He died October 25, 1937. The Poloson Ranch was made up of the Van Der Ende, Quilligan, Howser, Loder, and Carlin homesteads. Dan and Mae added another eight hundred acres located south of the ranch house. They bought this for taxes bringing the ranch size to twenty five hundred acres.

The Carlin homestead was south of the main ranch house and a mile beyond the Hauser place. The Vander Ende place was a mile west of the Carlin place. This homestead had a wonderful spring that in later years fed the fish pond Bert built.

Tjittes (Ted) Vander Ende was born March 31, 1886 in Wosterend, Netherlands. He came to the United States by boat. Ted settled in Chicago and left for Montana when the Flathead Reservation was opened up to homesteading. He made his way to Kalispell then took a boat to Polson. From Polson he walked over 25 miles to look at the homestead he would establish. After the Vander Endes sold the homestead to Jim & Klonda Howser they moved to Lonepine where they had a small place and ran the Lonepine store. Ted and Jessie White Vander Ende had ten children.

The Howser place was homesteaded by Jim & Klonda Howser about 1915. They bought the Vander Ende homestead in 1917. The home they built was a quarter of a mile from the main Poloson ranch house built by the Quilligans. The Howsers raised beef cattle and lots of garden produce including strawberries, and an orchard. They also raised turkeys and chickens. Jim was born December 3, 1988 and passed away in February of 1984. Klonda was born August 6, 1896 and died in September of 1982. When Dan and Mae bought their place in 1940 Mom lived in the house when I was a baby.

*Building the chimney for the fireplace at the
Howser house in Rattlesnake Gulch*

The Poloson ranch was located in Rattlesnake Gulch and it lived up to its name; rattlesnakes were everywhere. Three generations and numerous hired hands had many confrontations with rattlesnakes but to my knowledge no one was ever bitten.

Grace Murray Loder homesteaded on a parcel in 1912 that later became part of the Poloson Ranch. She taught school at the Rattlesnake School and told of killing numerous rattlesnakes as she walked through the sagebrush to the school. She married Robert Loder who had established a homesteaded nearby a year earlier. They had several artesian wells until too many wells were drilled and they stopped flowing. Robert's mother, Anna Loder, had a homestead next to Robert's. Their homes were fifteen feet apart with a walkway in between. The Loder homesteads were on the flat below the Howser place east of present day Highway 28.

Grace Murray Loder was the daughter of Reverend S.H. Murray. He ministered to the spiritual needs of the Lonepine community for a number of years. The Murray Memorial Cemetery was named after him.

Looking southwest from the Poloson ranch house. The Howser place is below the corral and in the distant left is part of the Vander Ende homestead. The Loder homesteads joined the Vander Ende place directly below the Howser place.

Dan and Mae built the sheep shed in 1935. Small pens called jugs were built inside along one wall. These were four by five feet just big enough for a ewe and lamb or lambs, and a person, usually Dan. Dan would hold the ewe with his head against her side while holding the lamb up to her teats to suck. If a lamb died and another was orphaned Dan would skin the dead lamb and make a "jacket" for the orphan lamb. The dead lamb's mother would accept the jacketed lamb. It takes a special person to work with sheep. Patience, knowledge, ambition, stamina, and dedication are necessary and Dan had an abundance of each. Dan's only rest during several weeks of lambing were cat naps in his favorite chair. The luxury of sleep in a soft bed had to wait until after lambing was finished.

Building The Sheep Shed

    The ewes and lambs were moved to a larger pen inside the sheep shed. When the lambs were old enough they were moved to a much larger area outside.

    The Shearing area of the sheep shed was built with a tall platform for filling wool sacks. The platform had a ring in the center that fit the opening of the eight foot long wool sacks. Each sack held the wool from ten ewes. Wool trampers, usually Fred Poloson and Paul Worth, would keep tramping the wool until the sack was filled, then the sack was sewn with paper twine. (Paper twine washed out of the wool when it was processed) Ears were left on each end of the sack when it was sewn so handlers could get a good hold. The sacks were stacked inside the sheep shed until they were shipped.

The cook house was built before the crew started on the sheep shed. Different cooks were employed during the busy years, and Mae, Marie, and Fay did their share of cooking too. Jack Gaston hired on as a cook during the 1930's. Jack was born April 7, 1884 and died in February of 1979. He is buried in the Murray Memorial Cemetery at Lonepine. Cattle Kate cooked for the crews during the 1940's. She always had a cigarette in her mouth so ashes were usually on the menu.

Cattle Kate

An Immigrant, a Homesteader, and Sheep

Marie's Star

1. Bunk House
2. Out House
3. Wood Shed
4. Cook House
5. Carlin House

Fay (left) Marie (Right) Truck Garages and hay yard in background. Mid 1930's.

Bert Poloson about 1935
Building the school bus garage. Bunk house,
Carlin house, and barn in background.

Bill Murray and Fred Harris Both worked at the ranch. Bill Murray also drove school bus.

The Poloson Ranch came to life every fall when the sheep were brought home from the hills. Hired hands and family were all busy caring for the sheep. The bucks were turned in with the ewes in early October. Gestation for a ewe is five months. Lambing would start by March 5th and was complete by the end of March. Shearing was next with docking of tails, castration, and dipping soon afterwards. By the end of May the sheep would be trailed to mountain pastures again.

Eddie Sorimpt and Louis Camile worked for Dan herding sheep summers. Eddie was from the Colville Indian tribe. He was born January 13, 1913 and passed away at Medical Lake, Washington in December of 1980. Louis Camile was from the same tribe. Louis was born February 22, 1890 and passed away in August of 1969 at Inchelium Ferry, Washington. Vic Pilgrun herded sheep all day long on horseback. Vic was born in 1884 and passed away October 20, 1959. John Arndt helped herd the Poloson sheep when he was seventeen.

Fred and Bert went with their Dad every summer during the 1930's and early 1940's. Both have had a life long love of the mountains that started in the sheep camps.

Charlie Hurst helped feed with a team and started driving school bus in 1936. Charlie was born February 2, 1911 and passed away at Spokane, Washington in April of 1987.

Fred Poloson and George Wells hauling hay

Fred, Bert, George Wells, and Lewis Mountjoy did most of the hay hauling. Baled hay replaced loose hay in the 1950's.

Bert Poloson and Lewis Mountjoy 1948 International

George Wells put the poles in for the four mile power line from the highway to the ranch house in 1948. George Wells was born

December 2, 1911 and passed away October 27, 2002. A gasoline power plant lit up very dim 32 watt bulbs in the sheep shed and ranch house before this.

Stacking Loose Hay

Fred Poloson 1938

Loading the wagon

Before 1935 hay was hauled to the ranch with wagons. Dan would winter the sheep in Valley View where hay was grown then bring the ewes home for March lambing. In 1935 Dan and Mae bought a 1935 International truck for hauling hay so the sheep could be wintered on the home ranch.

Other trucks were:
1939 Chevrolet that only lasted two years.
1941 white International that was a good truck.
1948 red International that lasted into the 70's.

Dan and Mae bought a D-4 Caterpillar in 1950. This was used to run the hay chopper, pull the road grader, and bring in winter wood.

Fay White International Early 1940's

Bringing in winter wood

Dan's International pickup. He owned several of these very tough pickups. Some of the terrain he would drive over was not for the faint of heart.

The depression years 1929–1940 were difficult for Dan & Mae. When Dan shipped his lambs to market by train from Plains he came home with $3200. Not enough to pay the banker, buy hay, and feed his family. World War II pulled the nation out of the depression. The demand for wool, lamb, and mutton gave Dan and Mae enough income to stay in the sheep business.

Mae made most of the children's clothing during the depression. She raised a huge garden every year at the upper spring. Fay said potatoes and strawberries took up the most room. "We picked strawberries by the bucket full. "Mae had lovely pear trees in the yard and the orchard by the Howser place had apples, pears, and plums. Mae, Marie, and Fay canned fruits and vegetables and made sauerkraut.

They raised chickens for meat and eggs. Fay and Marie took turns milking and caring for bum lambs. Summers were busy preparing for the winter to come. Dan, Fred, and Bert spent summers in the mountains with the sheep.

Fay said when her Dad and brothers were gone it was up to their mother to order chicken feed. The mail man would take the order then he'd drop the feed off at their mail box four miles from the ranch house. Fay said they would take an extra sack so the one hundred pound sack could be divided into two fifty pound sacks. This made it possible to lift it up on the horse and get the load balanced.

First Mail Box

Fay and Silver Belle (Notice the apron Fay has on; she's been cooking)

Marie & Bum Lamb

Bert & His Pet Magpie 1939

An Immigrant, a Homesteader, and Sheep

Grace On Ewe 1943

Dan Dipping Sheep

Poloson Sheep

Ewes On Pasture

Poloson Sheep Late 1930's

An Immigrant, a Homesteader, and Sheep

Dan & Fred With Pack String 1936

Dan & Fred On Baldy Cabinet Mountains 1933

Ranger Walter Robb and Dan Poloson St. Joe, Idaho

MARIE'S MEMORIES
MARIE: WOLF CREEK

I think my father was born with sheep. He said when he was 5 years old he was chasing a bear out of the sheep with a stick. When his brother Matt brought him over here from Romania, instead of going over into the factory in Detroit, he went to work in a packing plant in Chicago; there he met some sheep men that spoke of Montana and the big sheep ranches there. Dad ended up working at the Helena Valley Sheep Ranch near Wolf Creek, Montana.

During World War I he was foreman at the Helena Valley Sheep Ranch. I can remember him riding from the ranch to where we lived on Wolf Creek. He would put his hand on the yard fence and his horse, Prince, would jump in and he would stay in the yard all night until Dad would tell him he could jump out in the morning. I can remember I'd be asleep but in the morning I'd get up and tell Mom, "Well I know Dad's coming I can hear Prince's feet and his shoes on the rocks. Mom would laugh because it seemed like I was always right. Whether I dreamed it or guessed it, I don't know.

Anyway, Holly Herrin's wife had a Kentucky saddle bred horse she called Senator; when she got so heavy she couldn't ride anymore, she gave the horse to my mother. I remember Mom told me that when I was three months old I rode in a cradle on the right side, she rode side saddle, and when I was cutting teeth she said the minute she put me in the cradle and started riding I shut up. We would go with Dad when he tended camp, so I guess I started riding pretty young.

At Wolf Creek the train went through the backyard; when the work train came they often stopped because they liked my Mother's homemade bread and cinnamon rolls. They would get a drink of fresh water too. When Mom needed groceries a lot of times they'd take the list when they went back to Three Forks, where the train came from, and the next day when the work train came they'd bring our groceries, feed for the chickens, and kerosene for the stove. I remember at that time to us little ones a Hershey bar was a real treat. She'd break off two or three windows for Fred and I, and we'd eat our Hershey bar.

At that time most everybody drove horse and buggy or rode but I can remember big old square cars going by, I think they were called Buick's. Anyway, there were a lot of rocks up on the hill; Fay, Fred, and I liked to roll the rocks. Well of course when the rocks went down they went into the road and the cars would have to stop and move the rocks.

Our house at Wolf Creek was an old mansion. I remember there were a lot of steps to go up to get inside; you stepped into a big alcove then you went on in. There were halls and doors all over. There was a ball room too, and from the ballroom the marble steps went to the upstairs. To me, it seemed like the ballroom was a long way down from the veranda at the top of the stairs. Mom always worried about us falling off to the floor below. She worried about us breaking our necks on them, but we never did. We just used the downstairs. There was a fireplace in one of the rooms. The kitchen had a great big wood stove, oh gosh, it was huge. I remember it said "Majestic".

There was a well right in the yard by the front door that we carried water from. Can you imagine that close to that mansion and they didn't have water in the house? It had a bathroom but you had to carry a bucket of water in and flush it. That's better than going outside when it's below zero. I don't remember when Fred was born. I do remember Fred when he was about eighteen months old; down the track near our place was a little cabin and some people lived in it. They had a little boy named Bebe. Fred and I were playing and Bebe started to cry; Mom came running out, she said, "What happened to Bebe?" Fred said, "Well, Bebe wouldn't play so I falled Bebe in the ditch." Fred must have been about 4 at that time because he could talk.

There was a creek behind the house too. My brother Fred, who grew up to be a top welder and machinist, was standing on the bank; he was just learning to walk. Fred reached down to get a pretty rock and fell in on his head. When mom pulled him out he had both hands full. She said at that time "It looks like anything he wants he'll hold on to it."

When Bert and Fay were born, Grandma (Mary DeSchamps) stayed with us. Poor little Bert; he was born in September, and I remember Mom saying he never saw the sunshine till the next summer. Dad called him Bertie. "Be careful now with Bertie."

When Bert was, I think 5 or 6 after we moved over to the Quilligan ranch, we had old Dolly, she came with the ranch. She was kind of a chubby old mare, and he had his picture taken on Dolly standing straight up on her.

His little bare feet dug into her fat back.

GOING TO SHEEP CAMP

When we lived at Wolf Creek I remember going to sheep camp when I was old enough to ride. When I started I rode in a cradle on the sidesaddle. Mom would saddle Senator with her sidesaddle and tie my cradle on; Dad would saddle Prince then put his hand on the fence. Prince would jump out of the yard and we'd head for the sheep camp at Lincoln with all the supplies. When I got older I rode behind my Mom on Senator.

Sometimes Mom would drive the wagon filled with supplies. She always said she was a better teamster than she was a rider. The wagon had yellow trim with gray weathered wood. It was really bumpy to ride in. That country was steep and awfully rocky. Dad had us walking because the area was so steep when the wagon Dad was driving tipped over. He was more upset about the supplies he had to reload than the wagon cause he tipped it right back up on its wheels. He put his back under the side of the buckboard and just hoisted it right on its wheels again. Dad could lift an awful lot with his back. I don't know why he didn't have back problems but he never did. When we'd change hayracks from the wagon to the sled in the winter he'd just get under one end, two hired men under the other, and lift it up and set it over. My mom was always telling him, "Watch your back."

I went through there one time in later years, and to think when I was a baby I rode those hills with my Mom. Maybe the trail was right where the road went who knows as it had been so many years since Mom and I went to that sheep camp. If I remember, I think it was winter when I went through there.

I can't even remember where we were going.

WE MOVE TO RATTLESNAKE GULCH

In 1929, when I was 6 years old, Dad bought the ranch from Mike Quilligan; 1700 sheep that came with the ranch. We moved by train from Wolf Creek where the train stopped at Perma. Perma had a hotel with a large sign nearby that went over the road. The sign advertised Perma as the "Gateway To The Flathead Reservation, Camas Prairie, Camas, and Hot Springs." We were met at the Perma railroad station by men with teams, wagons, and trucks. They loaded all our stuff and took us on to the ranch. I think the first thing I noticed there was the rock fence clear across the front of the yard; someone said it would be full of rattlesnakes. We had never seen a rattlesnake. We were kind of curious but Mom put a stop to that real quick forbidding us to climb on the rock fence.

Mr. Quilligan was Irish. The Quilligans moved into a little house in Hot Springs but he often came out to the ranch to ride the white horse that he left with us; he called the horse Christmas. When Hot Springs had a parade we'd always see Mike on his white horse.

Mrs. Quilligan was really happy to be in town and away from the sheep. I don't think she was ever truly a sheep rancher's wife; she liked being in town. The Quilligans never had any children.

During the Depression Mike would come out and look around the place. I'm sure he was thinking, "pretty soon he'd have it back." He could sell it again because, I believe, this was the third time he'd sold it. But between us kids, Dad, and Mom we pinched pennies, worked long hours, and put up with a lot of discomfort and cold. Finally the place was ours.

JIM AND KLONDA HOWSER

In later years my father bought homesteads. One of the first he bought was the Loder place; the section with the schoolhouse on it, and then some state land. My mother bought a section that was in the middle of the ranch from Jim and Klonda Howser in 1940. It was right below the house; we pastured our horses and cows there separate from the sheep. She had a woven wire fence put clear around it.

Klonda was crippled. She was a maiden woman and probably in her seventies then. She was crippled because when she was a girl she got on a horse and someone slapped the horse on the rump and it threw her and she broke her hip. Of course in those days they didn't go to the doctor and she never healed right. Jim was very near sighted; he wore heavy glasses and drove an old Model-T. He liked to read like the rest of us. Their mailbox was right beside ours; he'd pick up the mail then read the newspaper as he drove home. I remember Slim Fields; he was kind of an Abraham Lincoln lookalike. He was sitting in the front seat with Jim. Jim went right on reading and steering; one wheel dropped over the edge. Of course that stopped the old car. He wasn't going very fast. Slim said they lifted it back up onto the road and Jim went right on reading all the way up the road. Of course I did my reading on the horse and the horse had sense enough to stay on the road.

Dad and Jim got in a fight over the road through Howser's place. Dad opened the gate and started through when Jim said he owned it, and Dad couldn't use it. It was county land so Dad had a right to use that road. Mom was out there yelling at them to stop fighting when Klonda came up with a shotgun and fired it; she stopped them. She thought that was terrible; two grown men fighting over a road. She let them know and Mom did too. Klonda used an old Maytag washing machine. We washed clothes by hand with a washboard. We didn't even have an old Maytag; everything was by hand. All through the thirties that I can remember Mom never had a washing machine. She didn't even want one. She didn't like the black smoke that she saw roll out of Klonda's which was pretty black and awfully smelly. Mom thought that would ruin any washing she did. Klonda was a lot like I was with my first old Maytag. I spent all morning jumping up and down on the pedal to start it. I was too tired to wash by the time I got it started but I had to wash anyway.

    Mom and I ironed. We used an old flat iron we heated on the stove. When it was hot enough we used a handle to hold it and iron; this was repeated many times until the ironing was all done.

HOMESTEADS, CHORES, AND SCHOOL

Dad bought the Vender Ende homestead; they didn't want to sell because it had that wonderful spring on it; they liked to come up there and get fresh water. But even after they sold to Dad they still came and got their water.

I think the Carlin homestead was the last place Dad bought. As Fred and Bert got older we needed extra room, so we moved the Carlin house about a mile then set it up next to our house. Fred and Bert set up living out there. We had the light plant for electricity. Mom said, "Be sure and turn the lights off every time you leave the room." Mom was putting clothes away and she happened to go into Bert's room. When she left she forgot to turn the light off; Bert came in there after school. I remember he yelled out, "Hey, Mom, some drip left my light on." He was just a little shaver then. Mom laughed and said, "Well I guess I'm that drip." She always had a sense of humor which was a good thing because we were $17,000 in debt, hay was $20 a ton, and sheep were a $1. a head. She had to have a sense of humor to make it. And I think it was her strong belief that we would make it along with her sense of humor that helped keep Dad going. I can remember him out there working all night long and coming in some mornings so tired; he would nap in his chair then go right back out and work all day long.

Before we left for school we did our milking then washed up and changed clothes. We had a driver, Bill Murray, that took us to school. He had a big old square Dodge. People asked how he could get through the bad roads. "Oh," he says, "I make her go." He would drive down through the flat and whenever there was a drift he'd dodge around it up and down the knolls finally getting us to the highway which wasn't much more than a two-track road. There were times when we walked home because Bill Murray got stuck. We always pulled a pair of corduroy pants under our dress; by the time we got home they would be so frozen they'd stand up by themselves. Dad would take the team down to pull the old Dodge out.

Usually we ended up walking from the old schoolhouse which was exactly a mile from our house. We could make it that far but from the school house on up the road would really drift; those little coulees where the little bridges were always drifted higher than the top of the old car.

When we got stuck Bill Murray would say, "yes gee vizz I think we got to walk." That was after he tried everything; forward then backwards; anything to get out. He would try pushing the car while one of us kept our foot on the gas. We learned how to drive at a very young age because of that. It was 8 miles to school and 4 miles of that was our road which was never really that good. Even though it was plowed it would drift full again. The men used four horses pulling a big grader to clear the road.

Dad loved workhorses; he had them all named. Dan and Prince were his favorites. They were both big brown horses; Prince was a little more black. Dan had brown streaks through his hair coat. I think they were in their twenties when they died. And I remember when Prince died that old Dan just stood around and by the next week he died. Bill Murray stopped driving bus about the time the county started paying so much for each of us to go to school. Then when the school district got a school bus nobody wanted to drive it with the long way they had to go. Charlie Hurst who frequently worked at the ranch took the job of driving bus. Charlie and his father were good friends of Dad's. The bus route was long; we'd go the 4 miles to the highway and then turn to the right and go all the way up into the main draw near Niarada to pick up students. We were only eight miles from the Lonepine School so this route made our trip a lot longer.

There were times in good weather that we rode our horses. When we took the short way by cutting across the flat it was about 5 miles. We had to build a garage for the bus; the men dug into the hillside then built a roof and garage door. After school we'd rush home hoping we could get the chores done so we could hear the

Lone Ranger or some of those classics on the radio. First off when we got home we changed our clothes then started chores. In the Fall we opened the gate to let the bucks in to feed them, and for the night. Then we had to milk the cows and do whatever things Dad wanted us to do. A lot of times we'd go get the work team or walk to get the cows. We had a Red Poll we called Old Gyp. I guess her name was Gypsy but we called her Gyp. When Bert got tired of walking we'd put him on Gyp.

He'd ride her all the way down to the barn. It was easy to find one of us on that cow. She didn't seem to mind us sitting up on her.

One time Bert really scared us all. He was on Bird, the old gray mare that came with the place. We were all galloping our horses and jumped the rock pile; Bert fell off. He was a little banged up but he wasn't hurt. Mom was so upset. Dad told her, "Well, he's got to get tough." Bert must have been 6 or 7 if he was that old; I was about 11. Bird was really a good horse most likely a purebred Morgan. She was really pretty and round. She was quite a horse even if she was old. Bird, Dolly, and old Baldy came with the place. Later on Mike Quilligan gave us his white horse, Christmas. We couldn't say "Slow as Christmas", because he was a fiery old horse, a big tall, heavy- set, white horse.

RATTLESNAKES AND OUR GARDEN

Mom had a big garden up by the spring and Dad had his potato patch. The garden was a little over an acre. Rattlesnakes were so bad; Louie Camille Lanto would go in there with a hook and take them out.

One cold morning Mom went up to work in the garden; as she stepped over the fence she heard a snake rattle. He was so cold he couldn't coil and strike. Mom backed up and stepped on another one. She said she got out of there and went right over to the cabin and woke Louie up. He went over and took them out. They were those big, short, fat ones about 3 feet long. They looked like they had a gopher in them all over but they were just fat.

The spring up by the garden was wonderful. The Howser place spring had watercress and all different little water things, and lots of frogs. There also was a nice spring on the Vender Ende place.

Mom irrigated the orchard from the Howser spring. There was an old, old orchard with huge pear trees and stuff like that; lots of plums and apples. I suppose Klonda and Jim's families probably planted it. Klonda's parents homesteaded the section that had the orchard in about 1913. They planted fruit trees then. Klonda was in her seventies when she sold to Mom in 1940. Jim died in 1928 and Klonda in 1944. Mom had a very nice orchard planted behind the house too. She planted rhubarb, horseradish, and asparagus. Dad liked horse radish so Mom would prepare that every year. Mom even grew a peach tree from a peach pit. Peaches were Dad's favorite fruit. That tree would produce several big peaches every year. Mom watered this area with water from the spring that was piped to the house from the cistern by the buck pasture.

HAY AND COLD WINTERS

Hay for the sheep, cows, and horses was hauled in by the trucks from the Lonepine Valley. The first truck was a Chevy bought in the early '30's and after that the White International. It was a big old bugger and cold blooded; so very hard to start. Frequently we would have to pull it with the team. By pulling it fast enough then letting up on the clutch usually the engine would start. The International had a long nose. Charlie Hurst said it took two blocks and another block to turn it around. Dad bought a red International in 1948. That's the one in the picture of the boys standing on top of the load of hay.

During the blizzard of 1936 we had snow over all of the fences. We could even drive the team and sleigh over top of the fence because the snow was frozen so hard. The sheep were down in a little hollow in the snow where Dad drove the sled in to feed. The snow was packed down in the feeding areas. The cattle were fed outside; the deer, elk, and the wild horses all came down to eat with the cattle. The winter of 1936 was so hard on livestock. I can remember sleigh riding all around on that snow. It's funny we had time to sleigh ride with all the work we had to do. Dad bought his hay from the farmers around Lonepine but they got so greedy that he started buying it near Ronan. In the early 1940's Dad trailed the sheep over to Howard Lulow's where they were fed during the winter then he would trail them home for lambing. Dad decided it was easier to truck the hay in and feed at the ranch instead of trailing the sheep so far. It was over 25 miles across country to the Lulow place. Dad bought hay from Lulow for years.

There were quite a few men who worked on our ranch. Fred Harris, Bill Murray, and Irvin Hurst, Charlie Hurst's father were three of the older men. For a while Fred Harris was Dad's partner until Dad bought him out. He came with us from Wolf Creek. Fred had worked with Dad on the Helena Valley Sheep Ranch so he knew us kids when we was babies. Fred was named after him.

When we moved here the sheep shed was on the side of the hay barn; it was just a short, low shed. Charlie, Dad, and Ikey Bender, a friend of Charlie's, built the shed at the end of the barn. It was clear across the end of the barn; they kept adding to it until the big sheep shed was built in the '40's.

The Quilligan ranch had a cabin by the upper spring the herder stayed in. When the herder was in the hills he had a tent and we used horses to pack his camp in. When I a young girl I could take the pack string into the hills to the herder. He'd unpack it then load the pack horses with meat or what ever he needed to send back. I'd go home and never lose a horse. Dad started me awfully young. He couldn't have if I hadn't loved horses and riding so much.

The cabin was near the water that came down to the corrals. The house water came from up on the hill where the buck pasture was. I remember when Dad and the hired men built the cow barn up at the spring. The cow barn was just slab sides and a flat top, mostly with branches laid across, and then straw on it which sheltered the cows; it also was a home to rattlesnakes. There was a little cabin there where the Indian herder lived. Louie Camille Lanto took over the Indian cattle herding. When we'd go up to the cow barn we'd see four or five rattlesnakes hung up. Louie would drip the oil (venom) in little containers. He got $35 an ounce. I think he was a Cherokee Indian. He had copper skin and blue eyes.

Louie wanted to give me a little black mare because I liked her so well, and she was a good jumper. I used to jump the 4 ft panels on her. Louie knew Mom would never let me take her as a gift, so he said we'd have a horse race and if I won I could have her. My little fat horse, Star, beat him by a long ways. He held the little black mare back so I could win.

There were wild horses back of the ranch that got used to seeing me on horseback. I was finally able to get them to come for oats. There were few fences which gave the horses a pretty big area to range in. It was common for farm horses to take up with the wild ones.

Bud Cheff, who grew up on the Flathead Reservation, mentioned the wild horses in his book, "Indian Trails And Grizzly Tales."

Some of my earliest spending money was made catching runaway horses for the farmers in the valley. When I coaxed the horses in with old Dolly half a dozen or more of the farmers saddle and work horses came in. Sometimes wild horses came in with them. The farmers would pay for catching their horses giving Dad a box of apples or something. Dad would pay me what he thought the apples were worth. Jess Miles came to the ranch In the early thirties before I was twelve; he showed me how to train horses so well that Dad said I was half horse. I could go in the corral with a 2 year old and in a couple of days I'd be riding the horse. Jess smoked Bull Durham; he could roll a cigarette with one hand while riding a horse. He had a way with horses; Jess frequently stayed at the ranch during the '30's and '40's. He worked with our ranch horses and Fay's Palominos and Arabs. His ability to break horses was really appreciated.

COOKING AND COOKS

Its surprising how Mom taught me to cook; how did we have time. Going to school along with milking before and after school took up most of my day. When Mom broke her ankle I was elected to the cookhouse. I was also herding sheep when one day I made the mistake of tying a colt I was riding to my father's rocking chair. He came around the corner kind of in a hurry and scared the colt, and it pulled the chair out the door. Dad caught the colt and luckily the chair wasn't broken. When I came in that evening the hired man had put a great big post in the ground. It was almost too big for me to get my arms around; it had a chain and snap attached to it. Dad said, "Here, now you snap this into your horse's halter. You leave my chair alone." Mom laughed; everybody laughed about that. I had to watch the pies I made. Even at 12 and 14 years old I was a very good pie maker. The men really liked pie. After the pies were done baking I'd set them in the window to cool, and of course it didn't have a screen or anything. Sometimes I'd end up missing one so Dad put a heavy screen around the outside of it to protect my pies. I always saved him a piece of pie at night during lambing because he'd come in at midnight to eat and at one time evidently the bus driver and my brother Fred had found where I put his lemon pie, and they left him some bread crusts I was saving for dressing. He was very upset about that; when he got through talking to them nobody stole his pie again. Dad and Fred both enjoyed lemon pie so I made it often. After Dad hired half a dozen men or more he built the cookhouse and hired a cook. I remember we had Miss Mosier. She wore eastern riding britches called drums so the men called her the drumstick cook. She was from Camas. Miss Mosier was a very dignified lady and a good cook. We had Helen Dahl; Gerald Dahl was her brother; he worked for Dad. John Bucheck's name sounded like "Boot Jack" so that's what he was called. He was a lumber camp cook before coming to the ranch; his meat pies were good except for the crust. The crusts were a disaster; the men could hardly cut them with their knives. Boot Jack made an agreement with me so as soon as I got home from school I made the crusts. Cattle Kate was a wild one. She dropped cigarette ashes in the cooking, and could cuss up a blue streak at the men if they made one complaint about her food. She didn't last very long and then Fay took over. There were usually six extra men when the shearers came. Dan and Dave Mortimer along with their father, and Charlie Comlin are all that I remember. I really liked them because they brought books for us. Every year when the Mortimers came they brought us something. One time it was apples from Yakima.

The men who worked for Dad appreciated the big cookhouse. They never left the table hungry. Men would winter at the ranch just for a bed and meals. Of course they had to earn both by working around the place.

LAMBING AND SHEARING

Lambing started in March. Us kids usually got the team ready and drove or rode them up to the haystack to load hay for the sheep and cattle. When the hay came in on the truck the team had to be there to pull the hay up onto the stack. Whenever I would ride up to the haystack I'd hop up on the feed box to get up on the back of the big horse then duck as we went out the barn door. The feed boxes were about 5 feet off the floor; they held oats for the horses. During the day Dad had 4 or 5 hired men that took care of picking up the newborn lambs. They would put the ewes in the jugs with their lambs. Ewes can forget they had the lamb or they would disown it. Dad or the hired man would crawl into the jug, hold the ewe against the wall, and help the lamb nurse. It was usually a fight. Most of the time this worked and the ewe would finally accept the lamb. Dad was usually the night man. This was a time of very little sleep. Bill Murray took the night shift sometimes to give Dad a rest. This was a very busy time and usually the weather was cold. Shearing was next then the ewes were dipped to protect them from parasites. I think Dad built the vat in the thirties. Bert was just a little shaver then. Helen Dahl took a picture of Dad that I'll never forget; he was bent over, in his bib overalls, pushing a sheep under the dip. He told Helen, "All you got was my hind end."

One of the men would push the ewe into the vat. Dad would push them under and they'd come up the walk at the other end. Oh, what a messy, dirty job that was. All of us smelled like sheep dip. We called it sheep dip in those days; we used it for cuts on horses too. It had a creosote smell; it could have had nicotine in it.

Ticks were a concern but I don't think worms were; we gave the sheep sulfur salt that came in 50 lb. blocks. It was rock salt or block salt with the sulfur in it. Us kids used to break off chunks of salt to lick before the sheep got to the blocks.

MAMALIGA

My favorite food that Mom fixed were her pancakes. She made those in different shapes for us. Bert liked his shaped like a turtle. Mom would give us sugar and cinnamon or syrup; anything we wanted to put on our pancakes. We used lots of butter which we churned.

Dad liked what he called Mamaliga; this was a corn meal mush made the way it was made in Romania. Mamaliga was a stiff corn meal mush that Mom could slice and fry. Dad would eat that with butter and syrup. Mom made this a lot when we were little. It was the old time corn meal that made it so good.

Makes 6 servings of Romanian mamaliga
Cook Time: 45 minutes Total Time: 45 minutes Ingredients:
- 3 1/2 cups water
- 1 1/2 teaspoons salt or to taste
- 2 tablespoons butter
- 1 cup coarse yellow cornmeal
- Sour cream (optional)
- Telemea or feta cheese (optional)
- Fresh herbs of choice (optional)

Preparation:
1. Bring the water to a rolling boil. Add the salt and butter, stirring to melt using a wooden spoon, add the cornmeal very gradually, while stirring constantly in the same direction.
2. Simmer over low heat, stirring frequently, until it thickens and starts to pull away from the sides of the pot, about 35-40 minutes. Serve hot.

3. NOTE: If desired, while Mamaliga is still hot, add more butter, cheese, sour cream and herbs. Mamaliga can also be served with a dollop of sour cream. Mamaliga can be poured into a pan. When cool, it can be flipped out onto a cutting board, cut into squares and sauteed in butter until crispy.

Mom made the best chicken; she'd cook it in its own gravy. It was so tender It would fall apart; add Mom's fresh baked bread and we had a feast. We had huckleberry jam when Dad or the herder picked them.

THE DEPRESSION

During the Depression years we had to wear our shoes a lot longer. Fred and I have crooked toes. Fred said his came from wearing a poor pair of shoes bought at the Mercantile in Plains. These years were very difficult. No one had very much money and what they did have was really stretched.

Mom made most of our clothes during the Depression. She had clothing she no longer wore that she would use to make clothes for us. When we left Wolf Creek we had plenty of clothes. Dad made good money at the Helena Valley Sheep Ranch. We had nice bedding and about everything we needed. But as we grew older we outgrew our clothes. I remember Mom taking her khaki riding outfits out of the trunk. She made jeans for Fred and Bert out of that material. Mom sewed everything by hand. She taught me how to sew and embroidery. When I was older I embroidered pillow cases and sold them at the Lonepine store.

We got our shoes from catalogs, the Mercantile in Hot Springs, or the Mercantile in Plains. The Mercantile in Hot Springs covered an entire block; it was completely destroyed by fire in 1931.

When times got better Mom would order clothing and household items from Sears, Wards, or National Bellas Hess. The latter was located in Chicago. They had the prettiest dresses for a dollar. Fay and I couldn't wait for their catalog to come.

Men would come and work all summer if Dad would let them stay through the winter. Phillip Straus was one of the men who stayed at the ranch. Phillip drove us to school sometimes. So many of the men were alcoholics; they would stay sober for months then go on a big drunk. Bill Murray took one vacation a year and spent it at the bar. He was a "reformed alcoholic". Dad talked about the time Bill hollered Whoopie, threw his hands up, and somersaulted off the bar stool.

Irvin Hurst's father, Albert Hurst replaced the bathhouse he leased from the Tribe with a stucco building and added a "mud bath" that his son, Irvin, managed. When the bathhouse reverted back to the Flathead Indian Tribe Irvin went to work for Dad.

In those days there weren't any jobs so getting through the winter was very difficult. People stole wood; they stole everything. Miss Mosier, who cooked for us, had so much wood stolen from her little house in Camas that she moved her wood into the house, covered it with her mattress, and used that for her bed.

If a person didn't have cash the stores couldn't afford to give credit. Dad was awfully lucky because McGowen Mercantile in Plains gave him credit. McGowen Mercantile also ordered in the wool sacks Dad used at shearing time. Dad had accounts at LaRue's Grocery and the Hot Springs Mercantile. Dad would buy warm clothes for the men that couldn't afford them. Dad believed in dressing warm. He'd tell Bert, "Now Bertie, put your overcoat on." Dad called a heavy jacket an overcoat.

Stores handled a lot of different items; harness, rope, farm and ranch equipment, clothing, and groceries. During the '50's Dad bought groceries and some supplies at the Lonepine Store. By then the cookhouse wasn't used; meals were prepared in the large, modern kitchen in the new house.

During those poor Depression times people would turn their horses loose, and some even turned their cattle out; they ran wild in the hills. The horses usually survived the winter but some cattle died in the gullies. The snow drifts were so deep the cattle couldn't get to the grass.

Dad always had enough hay for the sheep, cattle, and horses. Wool actually brought a fair price during the '30's and '40's, but sheep prices were awfully low; around a dollar a head. The weather was cold; '32 and '33 were mild but '34 was cold, and '36 was terrible. 40 below was nothing and the snow was so deep it covered all the fences. There wasn't any money and the winters were so cold. We were really lucky because we had our milk cows, chickens, and hogs. Mom never had a refrigerator at the ranch. She kept canned milk cool by setting it in cold water. Celery was kept in a bowl of cold water. We always butchered and cut up our own meat. Mom stored vegetables, apples, and pears in the cellar. She had a "cooler box" by the side of the house that kept meat frozen during the winter. Mom canned a lot of our meat before we had the deep freeze in the cook house.

Dad would butcher a fat lamb or a Wether. A Wether is a castrated sheep a year or two old. Home raised Mutton was good but Dad always said, "Don't let the wool touch the meat." When Dad would skin a sheep he would keep rolling the hide back so it wouldn't touch the meat.

When we butchered our pigs we used a block and tackle. First we'd hook the pigs hind legs to a singletree then hook the singletree to the rope that went through the block and tackle. This rope was hooked to another single tree that was attached to the horse's harness. By leading the horse forward this raised the pig up so Dad could butcher it. Dad would lower the hog into boiling water so us kids could scrape the hair off the hide. This made nice side pork with that wonderful rind to chew on.

Mom always had about 40 chickens, and she had ducks. Someone had given Mom a bunch of Mallards which are generally a wild duck. Mom thought it funny that these ducks never laid eggs. The white ducks were laying all the time. About three weeks after Mom's comment the Mallard ducks came down the hill from the Buck pasture followed by lots of baby ducks. Mom had close to a 100 baby ducks so we ate a lot of duck that year.

She used Paraffin to take the down off the duck after she had picked all the feathers. The paraffin was melted in the big kettle used to dip the duck. By straining the paraffin through cheesecloth she was able to save it and use it again.

We used a lot of cheesecloth for straining milk, mosquito netting, making lard, etc. Mom would cook pork fat and rinds until the fat melted then she'd strain it though cheesecloth so the lard was pure. The rinds would turn into cracklings and the fat would melt. Cracklings were a treat for us kids.

People used cheesecloth for netting over baby buggies so the baby would be safe from mosquitoes out in the yard. Cheesecloth was even used for bandages because it washed so clean and dried fast.

When we would buy cheese at the butcher shop it would be wrapped in cheesecloth. That is how cheesecloth got its name.

Macaroni and Cheese were a stand-by in the cook house especially with the sheep herders. Mom made it too. It was one of Bert and Fred's favorite meals. Mom used real cheese and lots of butter. The macaroni was bigger than what we have now. It cooked up nice and fluffy. I don't care that much for Macaroni and Cheese anymore; we had it so often when I was growing up.

The Depression continued until after World War II. During the Depression I earned some money by herding Indian Department cattle. I used that and what I made from bum lambs for school clothes. Mom was very frugal; she grew up during hard times so she knew how to make do with what she had. That's what helped Dad get through the Depression; that and the fact the bank wasn't about to foreclose when sheep were a dollar a head. With money so scarce we could go to a movie for 5 cents.

We kept the heifer calves from our milk cows to build the herd; we kept them in the section Mom owned below the house. Mom's brand was Bar MP. Dad's brand was KL Bar. Fay had the beautiful Lazy Anchor brand; we usually branded the horses with it. It was a small brand used on the left shoulder of the horse.

NICK AND ANNA LASCU

Anna Lascu had the most beautiful home but the house was only used at bedtime. When I helped Anna, we spent the day working. If I was out in the hills she would come with her pickup and lunch. Sometimes it was fried chicken; she was an excellent cook and believed in a person eating a lot. Anna used the cookhouse instead of the kitchen in her nice house.

Nick had made such a mess of her nice kitchen when he cooked spare ribs in the pressure cooker. Nick took a nap and forgot about the pressure cooker. It blew up spewing spare ribs all over the kitchen ceiling, walls, and floor. Nick left for sheep camp before Anna found the mess.

Anna would cuss Nick out something terrible. Nick was so quiet and withdrawn; sort of like he was scared. He'd go into the cookhouse where we always had a coffee pot on; he'd stay away from Anna. But when he left for Browning with the sheep they were talking again. Anna would say, Oh, my Nickie. I miss my Nickie." I think Nick realized how she was after living with her all that time. Anna said she lived with Nick for 10 years before she married him because her first husband was also named Nick, and he beat her. She wasn't taking a chance this time. Anna told me, "You never marry a man with a temper; he beat you." I was about 12 when she told me this.

In the early spring Nick took the sheep to the Duffy place. That was back of our ranch and bordered Indian land. Nick took the sheep to Browning in June. I'd check on Anna and often spent several days with her when Nick was gone. When it was raining I would ride my horse in their big sheep shed. It was so big it made the Guinness Book Of Records. The shed couldn't hold all of their sheep. Nick had it fixed up with "little jugs" to put the ewes in during lambing. Where these jugs were along the sides, if a person wasn't short, they would have to walk bent over.

I helped Anna in the garden. Anna had a straw hat on and she would tuck her dress in her pantywaist. She looked like a Chinese coulee worker. Anna built a dam for her water with a dirt mover that was pulled behind a horse. I drove the work horse and Anna handled the dirt scoop.

Albert Marquardt homesteaded by Highway 28 across the road from Nick and Anna's. When he closed his dam the water flooded the sheep shed. Anna was so upset she was going to sue him. Then she got to thinking; she could build a dam across the creek that would take away his water. She went ahead and built that dam. Albert came over to talk to her one evening, "Annie, I vant some water." Anna had the hose with spray nozzle nearby. Anna said, "You vant some water, huh?" Then she repeated, "You vant some water?" She kept looking at Albert; pretty soon she turned the hose on and said, "I'll give you all the damn water you vant right now." I thought this was so funny. Albert left without swearing at Anna. He got in his car, wiped his wet face with his sleeve, and drove home.

Later on Anna did open the dam so Albert could get some water. He hadn't sued her and she was happy that she could keep him from having water. Albert did have a windmill and could pump water for his cattle.

Anna was a beautiful seamstress; she made me a skirt and bolero that was just like I could have bought from a high-class clothing store.

Nick and Anna came from Romania. Nick came west and started working with sheep. Anna worked in hotels and restaurants; she did all kinds of woman labor, scrubbing, cooking, etc.

After Nick bought the ranch he needed a housekeeper and cook. Anna said Nick wasn't the kind who beat her or took her hard earned money. Nick was her third husband. She never spoke about her previous marriages except for the abuse.

Nick and Anna were here when we moved from Wolf Creek in 1929; their big sheep shed was already there. Nick rode horseback when he herded the sheep; he always had a couple of dogs with him. He either walked or drove his pickup when he was home. He had a little, old, blue Ford pickup. Anna had a pickup too.

Anna would drive her pickup across ditches, over rocks, and places a person would hardly take a horse. I'd see her coming up the hill bouncing over rocks and ruts. She'd bring lunch and we'd set on the tail gate and eat.

During lambing Nick had lots of help; way more than he needed according to Dad. Anna didn't cook for the crew; she was out in the sheep shed. They hired a cook during lambing and shearing. Anna was awfully hard to work for.

My first date was with Nels Frolan. He had a horse named Deuce that we rode to the dance. Anna gave him quite a sermon before we left and when we came back she said, "Oh, my baby, are you alright? He no bother you?"

SHEEP MEN AND RUSTLERS

One of the first sheep men I remember was Ben Sickler. He had the nice fish pond where us kids could catch trout to take home for mother to fry. Ben Sickler lived near the Niarada store. The Swishers hauled water from the big spring near Sickler's; that is where Sullivan Creek starts. Louie O'Connel had around 2000 head. His place was northwest of Niarada in the foothills by the road that goes to Kila. They called this area Hog Heaven.

I can't remember so many of the early sheep men. I do remember this though: Dad had asked me to take the cows down to the Vander Ende place. My horse started acting funny and I could smell cigarette smoke. I told Mom, "when that happened my hair almost pushed my hat off!" The smell was coming from the timber right above me. I had heard a truck come in and that scared me even more. I started back towards the house but something told me not to take the road. I went up into the trees and rode along the hill.

The next day I saw tire tracks on our road by the Vander Ende spring. Dad drove over there a lot so I wasn't sure until I went into the old Vander Ende house. The dog started sniffing and scratching around the floor boards. I could see a strip of white under one of the boards so I lifted the board up; there were Hereford cattle hides buried under that floor. These came from the Indian owned cattle. I don't know how many there were because they were really packed down and covered the ground under that floor. Thats when I knew the tire tracks were most likely made by cattle rustlers.

I forget how many days later Art Malm and Gerald Doll were thrown in jail for rustling. The man who ran the frozen food locker was fined for his part in the rustling.

Gerald's sister, Helen, cooked at the ranch. She was a good cook and didn't even mind Mom's roosters attacking her when she went after water, but they were awfully hard on her stockings. Pete was a Plymouth Rock and Ebenezer was a Wyandotte. Sunshine was a Buff Orpington. Sunshine was gentle but Ebenezer and Pete had tempers.

Jess Miles was accused of stealing a horse; he took off for the hills with the sheriff and his deputy after him. Jess jumped his horse into the Lonepine Reservoir and swam across into the hills by Annie McDonald's place. He got as far as Reno, Nevada where he was arrested and sent back to the prison in Deer Lodge, Montana. The horse was confiscated and hauled back to Hot Springs. As Dad said, "It cost four or five times what the horse was worth to get him back." Jess swore he'd earned the horse as wages but the owner swore that he had stolen it.

McDonalds' lived across the reservoir along the hills west of Lonepine.

Annie was the widow of Angus; she was half Indian and Angus was Scotch.

BERT AND FAY: HERRON RANCH

Dad worked at Herrin Ranch near Helena where they had 8 bands of sheep or close to 8000 head. Dad was the camp tender for the Herrin Ranch. This didn't prepare Dad for the time the sheep got on a cattle rancher's land which was near Herrin's range.

The rancher had gathered the sheep and corralled them; when Dad found out what happened he asked the rancher what he wanted. The rancher wanted to be paid before he'd release the sheep. Dad and one of Herron's sheep herders went in that night and opened the gate to the corral. The sheep all came out. Dad & the herder pushed them as fast as they could back to home range. The next morning the rancher showed up with four hired hands. Dad was not much for shooting since he grew up in Romania where citizens were not allowed to own guns. Dad asked the herder to take the gun they had in their camp; he wouldn't so it was up to Dad to handle the gun. When the rancher and his hands were 6 or 7 feet from Dad and the herder Dad said, "That's far enough!". They stopped, turned around, and left.

Dad & Mom bought their own ranch from Quilligans in 1929. The sheep came with the place. They moved from Wolf Creek to Perma by train then trucked their belongings across Camas Prairie to the ranch. Art Kluzen and others helped them. They had no livestock, just personal belongings to move. Bert was 2, Fay 3, Fred 5, and Marie 6 when the Poloson family settled in Rattlesnake Gulch near Lonepine and Niarada, Montana.

COWBOYING, GARDENING,. AND SCHOOL

FAY:
I can't recall Wolf Creek except for being kids and throwing rocks at cars; we called the cars little devils .

When I was about five I was riding a little white mare named Dolly while Dad was fixing fence. Dolly began to jump around but I managed to stay on. I didn't fall off so I'm now a real cowboy.

Mom had chickens and a big garden by the spring three quarters of a mile east of the house. There was a sheep corral and a small building by that spring. We picked buckets of strawberries from our huge garden. An established orchard was below our house by the Howser place. We had pears, plums, apples, and cherries. Mom had a small orchard and garden on south side of house close to buck pasture. There was a spring in that corner of the buck pasture Mom irrigated from. Mom would walk back and forth through the garden with a hoe after weeds, and once in a while a rattlesnake. As a little girl, I spent a lot of time picking potato bugs. We canned a lot of fruits and vegetables, made sauerkraut, and stored root vegetables in the cellar. To wash clothes we put a tub on stove, heated the water, and scrubbed clothes on wash board.

The Carlin house was moved over by our house when Fred was 14 in 1938. The barn was on the place and Dad had a sheep shed built onto the barn; a lean to with a metal roof on the north side. There were some small sheds housing a blacksmith shop, a light plant, and a tack building. That held pack saddles, camp tent, stove, camp utensils, etc.

We had a woodshed and a bunk house. There was a big black walnut tree by the wood shed. That's where Alice and Gracie were busy cracking walnuts when Old Shep bit Alice on the nose. The bus garage was built in 1936. Charlie Hurst had the bus route from the ranch to Lonepine School. When August Magera took over driving we kids had to walk a mile to catch the bus. The truck garage was built in the early '40's.

The Rattlesnake Gulch School, about two miles from our house, closed several years before we moved there. Homesteaders children attended the old school after their families settled in the area. At one time there were 29 families; we have no idea where they all homesteaded. The Loders, Howsers, VanderEnde's, and Carlins were some of the families. The upper place where we had our big garden may have been part of Quilligan's place or an older homestead. A person had to have water or they couldn't raise anything. There were at least six springs on our place.

We all went to school at Lonepine. Fred was the only one who graduated High School. Fred was outgoing and enjoyed school. Bert was bored with school. I quit after the eighth grade and Marie was married at seventeen.

WRECKS

We had a lemon pie catastrophe when Marie lived in Hot Springs. She had baked a lemon pie and dropped it as she was taking it out of the oven. We scooped it up and ate it anyway. Gracie was a couple years old and she helped us eat it.

When Gracie was about 3 years old she ran away down the lane with her light colored hair bouncing as she ran; she was leaving home. It wasn't very long and she decided to come back.

I can still see the horse running with the stove dragging behind. Gracie was 7 or 8 when this happened. She was supposed to be leading the horse that ran away. I met Gracie by the gate; she was too small to get off and on the horse yet. Gracie said, "every once in a while I'd see a frying pan ". Dad needed a new camp stove and cooking utensils.

Cattle Kate cooked for the lambing and shearing crews in the cook house; she wasn't a very good cook and always had a cigarette hanging from her mouth with ashes dropping on the floor, and frequently in the food she was preparing. Kate would insist that I eat but I could not eat her cooking! Kate didn't stay long. I took over the cooking after Kate left.

Nick & Anna Lascu were already sheep ranching on the place next to the ranch Dad & Mom bought in 1929. Nick's outfit was one of the largest in the area. His sheep shed was 120 feet wide and 500 feet long and the second largest in the world. The shed was tall enough in the center that Arvid Kopp could drive a truck loaded with hay into it. There was enough room to stack the hay inside the shed for winter feeding. The Swisher girls and I used to ride horseback through it; it was big! During the summer I often worked for Anna washing dishes and weeding the garden.

WATER, HIRED MEN, AND ELECTRICITY

BERT:
Water ran all the time because of good springs with lots of water pressure. First, water was put in to the sheep shed. I can't remember his name but the guy who caught the big Sturgeon out of Flathead Lake used his D-4 cat to dig the water line to the shed. We bought 2500 feet of inch and a half pipe from Weisman then we had to thread it. When we put water in to the house we dug that line by hand. Our water was on gravity feed and we had plenty of pressure at the house. I was about 15 yrs. old when I made the water tanks for the corrals by hollowing out logs and closing the ends with concrete .

Jack Gaston worked at the ranch during the early '40's. His doctors had told him he didn't have long to live–6 months, so he sold his farm and everything he had except his team and wagon. 6 months later he's still alive and his doctor is dead. Jack Gaston lived to be ninety three. He cooked at the ranch when the cook house was a very busy place. Jack Gaston is buried in the Murray Cemetery at Lonepine.

Art Cluzen worked at the ranch for years. He'd drive us to school and did a lot of work for Dad. He was a small, quiet man and talked real slow. Art was driving his old car going to Spokane when he came to an intersection, hit the ice, and spun clear around. While he was in the intersection he said, "along came a car about 60 miles an hour then another car came from the other direction 60 miles an hour!" He did make it to Spokane. When he worked for Dad he stayed in the bunkhouse at the ranch. Art never did get married .

FAY:
A young man named Reynolds came to work at the ranch. He was studying to be a lawyer so when he wasn't working he was

studying the many books he brought with him. One day as he was fencing the buck pasture a roll of wire got away and rolled down the hill; he was running down the hill after it hollering " Whoa, Whoa, Whoa." Dad thought that was the funniest thing he'd ever seen.

By 1948 we had electricity. George Wells put four miles of power poles in; the power company furnished the wire and poles. That was the year the new house was built. Mom wouldn't move into it. She said she'd done her work and besides that she didn't like the slippery floors in the new house.

TRIP TO BROWNING– AREA SHEEP RANCHERS

BERT:
Nick Lascu summered his sheep North of Browning; he trailed to the Marion branch rail line then shipped them to Browning by train. Nick did that every year from his place near Niarada. I went with him the one time to drive the truck to Marion. We didn't help load the sheep but got them to the stock yards then left with the truck for Browning. Nick was a very poor driver; he could shift up but could not shift down. He'd wait until the engine died then put the brakes on and holler, "Boy, Boy, put 'em rock behind the wheel!" Nick had about 3,000 head of sheep. It was easier to run bigger bands in open country unlike the mountains where the herder couldn't see all of them. It takes a good herder to keep an eye on them in the mountains. I spent a few days in camp with George The Greek but I wanted to go to Shelby. For some reason Nick wouldn't go for that but I had a 37 chevy car so I went to Shelby anyway, and went to work as a laborer on a railroad siding filling pot holes, etc. I was just there a few days.

There were other sheep ranchers in the Lonepine & Niarada area. Harry Burgess had some sheep. Ira Baxter had a small bunch. There were several Baxters'; Chuck, Ira, and Hank. Dad would ship their wool with his. Argos had 6 or 7 hundred head. Dad took their sheep to the mountains with his one summer; that was a mistake! Too many sheep in a band just doesn't work. Charlie Bracket had a couple hundred head; Bert Young also had a couple hundred head. Bud Matt lived near Kerr Dam and ran a few sheep there.

A man named Fairchild owned the Polson Sheep Company in the '40's. He had 4 or 5 bands. Fred worked for him one season packing camps and herding sheep. Fairchild went out of business in the mid '40's. The Shanno Ranch near Dixon had a small herd of sheep. They would trail them through Dad's ranch and on to the hills for summer pasture. Claire Sheldon bought some sheep from Dad. Claire talked Tom King into bum lambs for the kids; he told Tom the kids will like them. Rosie (Swisher) King ended up taking care of them.

Bill Murray and Fred Harris worked on the ranch. Bill Murray helped in sheep camp, during lambing, and drove school bus. My brother, Fred Harris Poloson, was named after him. Fred Harris lived in Mosier Gulch. Mosier Gulch was about a mile NW of Camas in open country. Dad had a place leased there and Fred Harris lived on that place. This was in the early '30's. Poloson mail came out of Camas for years. John Rhone had a place there; Edna Gannaway had a newspaper office there; the Hot Springs paper.

There were a couple of houses there and a blacksmith shop .

TRAILING SHEEP AND HUNTING BEAR

We'd camp overnight near Camas when we took the sheep to the mountains. The camps were every 10 to 15 miles. We'd herd the sheep right through Camas following the highway then through rough country around the lake staying off the highway. There was a swamp on one side and the lake on the other; we went around the end of the lake then cut across country. There wasn't a road there at that time. An old logging camp had been in that area; some old trucks were still back in there. We camped at the end of Dog Lake. The next morning we cut across from there and came out north of Plains. Another camp was near Bert Young's place along the Thompson River. We pretty much followed the road through some rough country and meadows. We'd camp close to the creek or cross and camp just off of the Thompson River Road. That road comes up from Thompson Falls. We camped once more on our way to Fishtrap creek. We had 2 bands, a 1,000 head each. Dad pastured in the Fishtrap Lake area and also in the Thompson River country near the Lookout. That was all rough country.

When Dad went to the St. Joe he followed the same route; Mosier Gulch, Dog Lake, then staying at the Plains stock yards over night. We couldn't follow the highway so we went along the county road and crossed the bridge at Plains. The next day we trailed on to Swamp Creek; there were meadows along the way. We dropping down onto the cut off road (Highway 135) and camped in that area. This route came out near St. Regis.

From there we trailed through Superior. From Superior we headed towards the Lost Lake and Bonanza Lakes area. We'd camp there then move the sheep into the St. Joe River country. That area had a Ranger Station, Lookout Tower, creeks, and lots of high mountain meadows.

Black bear were plentiful; they would follow and kill sheep. Eddie Surempt, Dad's herder, killed 37 bear in one summer. I don't know how many Fred killed but it must have been 100's. Johnny Hart went with us one season. He said, "I sure hope I can kill a bear this summer so I can tell Charlie I killed a bear." The second day out of Plains he killed 2 bear and ended up killing 17 black bear that summer.

Fred was the bear hunter. He was up in the Buffalo Bill area with his rifle at his side; all of a sudden in the open, 75 yards away, a bear came into sight. Fred grabbed his gun and the bear went down. Fred was fast and also a dead shot. Dad had no fear of bear; one time he hit a bear on the head with his gun because he was out of ammunition; this happened over in the St. Joe. Up in the Fishtrap Dad killed a young bear then took the pack horse out to bring it in. He and George Wells got the old bear up on the horse; the horse was quiet until he saw the bear then he blew up and bucked the bear off.

Dad had a sheep dog named Tippy; he had a white tip on his tail. He was a good sheep dog and he would also chase bear. It was getting dark when Tippy treed a bear. Dad was afraid to let the bear stay there for the night because he'd come down later on and kill sheep so he shot the bear. Tippy was intently watching that bear and didn't get out of the way in time; the bear fell right on him. Tippy was in bad shape for quite a while and never did fully recover.

FAY:
One time we camped under a tree because it was raining and cold. I was about 7 and Bert 6. Lightening had struck a tree and started a big fire. Bert and I were riding double and we were scared but we didn't cry! Dad set up camp where we stayed over night. The next day we rode on to the main camp. Bert and I spent several weeks in camp during the summer. We would pick wild onions, ride our horse, and explore the hills. We wanted Dad to put wild onions in our pancakes but he wouldn't do it.

BERT:
Bill Murray had gone to the Young place to pick up salt for the sheep and eggs for camp. He packed the eggs in hay inside a bucket

so they wouldn't break. Dilly, the pack horse, was a little spooky although he was a good pack horse because he wouldn't bump into trees with the packs. When Bill got to camp he took the saddle off the horse he was riding, laid it on the ground, and looped Dilly's lead to the horn. This was before he unpacked the eggs & salt. If anything moved Dilly would shy; before Bill knew what was happening Dilly had backed up, and that saddle moved! Dilly stepped back again and the saddle jumped at him. He took off down the trail with blocks of salt and eggs falling behind him. When Dilly came back to camp he didn't have the pack saddle on. Soon after this happened Dad came into camp. He'd found the pack saddle with the lining all torn up. Fifteen eggs survived out of eighty one!

In the fall we would cut the lambs from the ewes near Bert Young's place. We'd leave a few old ewes with them and trail them into Plains to the stockyards to be shipped east on the train. It was a job moving the lambs from Young's to Plains; they wanted to go back to the ewes. The main herd was pastured for about a month in the Fishtrap area then we followed the same route home.

LOST WITH LOST SHEEP

When I was about 14 Dad and Fred were up in the Heavenly Peak country with the ewes. I had stopped at Bert Young's while looking for some lost sheep. A thunderstorm came up and it was kind of cool. I had no bedroll so when it got dark I just slept under a tree. Come daylight I could hear a couple of guys coming up the trail; they were smoke chasers looking for a fire someplace. They stopped for a bit then went on .

I finally found the lost 50 head of sheep. I had no choice but to start taking them back up to where Dad and Fred were with the band which was about half way up the Fishtrap from the Thompson River, Fishtrap cabin, and Dudley Peak. I'd never been up in that country. My horse had been without feed for two days so I picketed him where he could get some grass and took a nap. When I woke up no horse! I hung my saddle in a tree hoping the porcupines wouldn't get it then waded across the creek herding the 50 head across too.

When I found the trail of Dad's sheep I'd came to a place about 6 feet wide with lots of brush and timber. I couldn't get the sheep to move so bedded them down and headed on to Dad and Fred's camp. I didn't see the trail and made the mistake of turning right; had I turned left it was less than a mile to the camp. The trail l took looked more used so I ended up going clear around the mountain. On the way back I walked over to a ledge for a look; the sheep camp was about a mile straight down ! There was no way to get down those steep cliffs so I had to go down and around. When I got to camp I told Fred and Dad about the sheep and finally had something to eat. I hadn't eaten in all that time but it was slow moving with the sheep so I didn't use a lot of energy. Fred saddled up two horses and we went after the sheep. Another thunder storm came up but Fred had a tarp we slung over a tree branch and spent the night there. We went after the sheep at daylight and moved them on up to camp; as we were going back up we found my horse. He was young and didn't know where to go or he might have headed for the ranch.

We were coming back from the Thompson River country; I was driving the truck hauling a big brown jumping horse Dad had. We stopped at McGowans store in Plains. Dad had this horse tied in the truck; the rack was about 5 feet high. When we came out of the store there wasn't any horse, just a halter hanging over the side ! Some guy saw him jump over the rack and leave. We had no idea how the halter came off without breaking his neck. The horse headed off towards Hot Springs and home. Jake Johnson had raised him; we couldn't hobble his front legs or he'd still jump and be gone. Dad finally sold him to Claire Sheldon. Claire never had to open a gate; he'd ride up and the horse would jump over the fence or gate.

MUTTON, MESSY STREET, AND THE LAW

Ranger Ashley Wyman had a son 10 or 11 years old. The Ranger would check on sheep outfits. Dad always invited visitors to dinner if they came into camp at noon, but he had deer meat cooking this time, and it wasn't hunting season! Dad became very nervous and took me aside; I told him this Ranger was okay. Ranger Wyman's son Larry said, "This is sure good meat." Dad said, "It's mutton." Nothing more was ever said about it.

Over 40 years went by with Larry retiring from the St Mary's, Idaho Forest Service. Larry found my phone number when he was in Plains and called; I asked him if he recalled eating deer meat? Larry said that after they left camp his Dad told him it was venison. After talking to Larry I called his Dad. When I worked for the Forest Service he was in charge of the area I packed into. I asked him if he remembered eating deer meat in sheep camp years ago. We had a nice visit.

At that time we trailed all the sheep to the stockyards then cut the lambs out, and trailed the ewes back up into the Thompson River country. This particular time the city had just fixed up the streets. The sheep were in pens all night. We moved them out at dawn; the only way out was right down main street. They made quite a mess of the street. We were about a mile out of town when the Deputy Sheriff showed up. He asked, "Who's sheep are these?" Dad said, "Johnson, the banker." The deputy left without comment.

During the depression a banker had to go along and hope the next year was better. This was standard during the '30's and into the early '40's. I don't think Dad got out of debt until the '50's. When he shipped the lambs in the '30's he got 6 cents a pound! Ralph White was the lamb buyer the year the sheep messed up the street; that year Dad got 7 cents a pound in Plains.

THE REAL WORK BEGINS

We brought the sheep back to the home ranch in September. The bucks were put with the ewes in October. Lambing started the 5th of March and lasted at least three weeks. Dad hardly slept except to catch a short nap in his chair. Baby lambs are fragile especially in the cold. Some ewes would not claim their lamb or their lamb would die. When that happened Dad would skin her dead lamb and put that hide, as a jacket, on an orphan lamb; by smell the ewe would think it was hers. Dad knew every bit of the sheep business and could pick out the right ewe by sight.

Dad bought hay from the farmers in the valley when he was using loose hay. Leo Mountjoy, Fred, and I became masters at putting huge loads on the old International trucks. Dad always had Internationals because they were tough and held up when driven in very rough country. He bought alfalfa hay for the ewes and cattle. The ranch had a D-4 Caterpillar with a pulley which ran the belt to the hay chopper. Dad chopped the alfalfa for the ewes so there wouldn't be any waste of the stems. The chopped hay increased the ewes' nutrition which helped them nurse their lambs. Some ewes had twins and triplets so milk production was very important.

Docking, dipping, and castrating were done in early April. Dad castrated using his teeth because that had the least risk of infecting the lamb. Docking was done with a heated chisel. To dip, a man would push the sheep into a narrow vat; as they swam through another guy would make sure their head was dipped. The dip was made out of a creosote mixture. The concrete dipping vat was about fifteen feet long and two feet wide with an exit ramp on the end.

Shearing was done as soon as the weather was warm usually in late April. In the early days a crew of eight lead by Jess Mortimer came to the ranch. They could shear a lot of sheep and were done in a couple of days. When the big outfits shut down Red Larson and his two brothers from Wenatche, Washington would shear. The Lasons had an apple orchard in Wenatche. Each would shear 180 head a day; they were done in 5 or 6 days. Some older guys could only do 50 head a day so 180 a day required a lot of strength and skill. Before electric clippers motor powered clippers that were on the end of long lines jointed for easy movement.

The fleece were tied with paper twine so it could be washed. Dad bought a special twine so when the wool was washed the twine would wash out. Fred and Paul Worth tramped wool. Paul was from Hot Springs. The sacks held three hundred pounds each and were tied on the ends so ears would stick out for hand holds. The sacks were closed with heavy cord using a curved needle. We used a rope to help lift the sacks onto the truck. A load was usually 35 sacks or about 10,500 pounds. We usually had at least 2 loads. Dad shipped from Polson and Plains. I hauled mostly to the railroad in Polson but sometimes to Plains. The wool buyer had people there to load the rail cars.

FRED AND I AFTER RANCH LIFE

I took a trip down to Arizona. While I was there I ran cat moving soil into mounds for cantaloupe planting. When that job was finished the boss took me to the big rodeo in Tucson.

Before I was drafted into the Army in 1945 I packed for the Forest Service in the St. Joe. When I was eighteen Uncle Sam didn't waste any time drafting me. Fred took over my pack string; he'd been shoeing horses and mules in Glacier Park. When I came back in April of 1947 I went back to my job in the St. Joe. Fred and I both went to work in Glacier Park in 1948. Bill Yennie was the forest ranger then .

Fred blacksmithed and packed; he took the tough jobs moving lumber, ties, plywood, and other building materials into the back country of Glacier. He was really good at this besides the shoeing and blacksmith work. Fay came up to park every weekend. Park Management was a different system with a different type of people then, and as long as there were no fires we could ride where ever we wanted too.

We chased Indian horses out of the park; they were not allowed. We'd chase them out and they'd be right back in a few days later. I was packing out of St. Mary's in the eastern part of the park. The Blackfeet Reservation borders much of the east side. A man named Guy lived on the edge of the park and had horses; the Jensen kids had horses too. Adolph Opelka was the ranger then. A Chicago guy named John was the ranger before him. Not knowing anything about Guy's horses and their repeated entry into the park, John penned the horses up in a corral. He called Guy and said, "I've got your horses in the corral so come and get them." Guy said "them is my horses, you just feed them good." He wasn't about to come into the park because he'd be arrested.

Grizzly bear may have been in Glacier but I never saw any on the highway or anyplace else. Glacier had plenty of black bear. I shot at a black bear to scare her away but hit her. November had brought 6 inches of new snow and she dropped right there in the snow! I had hoped she'd go off and die but all she could do was move her jaws. I cut her throat with a knife Fred had made; there was blood all over. I had to wait until dark to back the car in and get that bear in the trunk. I took her out a ways to a place without a guard rail along a steep bank and dumped her. The ravens came to scratch around in the blood where I'd shot her so I put a box over the blood to hide it until nightfall. One guy said he'd have done the same thing and would have helped me load it!

I had a horse we called Curly Bear; he was out of Marie's black mare. Curly Bear was a bay and curly all over. I really liked Marie's black mare. Billy Andrews, Fred, and I each had two horses; I had Curly Bear and a big brown gelding that wasn't the best saddle horse. If one horse was missing we'd have to replace it so that's how we ended up with the big brown. He was a big, dumb horse but I'd never had any trouble with him until but one day when I was leading a mule string packing plywood for Two Medicine. I had the pack string ready when the rope got under my leg. The Chicago ranger was with me so he observed what happened next. Big Brown started bucking; he went about twenty feet across the road and back again. We made two rounds like that. When he'd come down on the pavement he was really rough! The first round the Chicago ranger sat on his horse with his mouth wide open. So Big Brown got a reputation!

We were going into a camp about six or seven miles in. This Chicago ranger needed a horse and wanted me to have a horse ready for him. I told him he could have Big Brown. The Chicago ranger fired me on the spot! I packed up and left walking back to the ranger station. The "word" got out so Fred, another packer, and other park employees said they were quitting. The District Ranger showed up and he stood up for me. I was off work about three days is all.

A job in Yellowstone Park came about when I was going through that country seeing the park. I stopped and talked to dude rancher who was looking for people for a trail crew. I had my saddle and gear in the car so I put in for a packing job. The guy in charge of packing was a good friend of Don Wyman's from Glacier, In a few days I had the job. After he hired me he said, "I was one of the best packers he'd ever seen." He'd packed for over thirty years and started in the twenties so he knew a good packer when he saw one. I lead four pack strings that year. The next year I went to work on road crew then did some drag line and back hoe work. The back hoe was a cable back hoe in those days. I was there until November of 1951.

While I was working in Yellowstone I saw one grizzly. She came into the campground; she was about two years old. Betty and I had our trailer on one end of camp; the rangers house was down below us and a bunk house was nearby. The campground had outdoor bathrooms. I came back from the bathroom and saw this bear with her head in the garbage can. I took off for the car when the bear got down deeper into the garbage can. All at once she came up out of the garbage can and turned towards me. I he went around the side of car and peaked around corner. I didn't see the bear so I thought I could make the other side of the car, and I might be able to open the door! I opened the door, got in, and went home. That same bear came up by our trailer; we couldn't get to the the outhouse or anything. I had a twenty two pistol. She was about fifty feet from the trailer on the door side. When I saw her coming I opened the door and shot from inside the trailer so the shot couldn't be heard. Betty and I managed to pull and roll her into the car trunk. A bear's hide moves so this was quite a job. We hauled her to an out-of-the-way place and got rid of her.

I moved back to the ranch near Lonepine where we had a few head of cattle. I started a logging business and had several trucks. We built a nice shop on the ranch where I rebuilt heavy equipment. I spent the last fifty years buying, repairing, selling, and renting heavy equipment. Betty and I were divorced in the early seventies. Grace and I have been married over forty years. Grace took care of the book work, our home, and beautiful yard.

Fred was a blacksmith in Yellowstone shoeing pack horses and mules and repairing equipment. Yellowstone wasn't as nice as Glacier. Fred went to work in Alaska so in nineteen fifty two I decided to work there. Fred drove the huge dump trucks and I ran different construction equipment building roads. When I came back from

Alaska I went to work in Mt. Ranier Park running a crane clam bucket cleaning up along retaining walls. Betty's sister had married to a guy that was working there. I worked there until November when weather got bad.

Fred was in Alaska for two years and worked in a blacksmith shop most of his second year. Fred worked on missile sites around Great Falls then on a dam in Washington. His wife, Ann, was always busy cooking, no matter where they lived, as she was a wonderful cook. In the early sixties Fred started working at local shop in Columbia Falls. He started doing contract work and built his own shop. Fred could build or repair anything out of iron. He spent his retirement making toy working cranes, shovels, and other types of construction equipment as well as axes and knives.

ERNESTINE MARIE POLOSON

Marie married my father, Clarence Galen Baker, in 1939. I was born the following November. They divorced when I was 8 months old and Marie married Warren Debs McBroom in 1942. Alice McBroom Kranzler was born July 23, 1943.

Debs was an excellent rider. I watched him ride a bay gelding named Cody. Cody blew up on a steep hillside; the hammer, staples, etc. flew everywhere but debs rode Cody until he finally quit bucking. Debs and his friend, Ronald Tibbets had been training remount horses for the Army when Marie met him. I believe of all the regrets my mother had was her divorce from Debs in 1949.

Debs & Marie purchased the Tennessee Walking Horse stallion, SilvertipRickey in 1947. That same year they bought Richardson's Honey Chile thus Marie's breeding program began.

Marie trained Rickey and he was absolutely the best horse I have ever ridden. He could out walk all the neighbors horses, and he was an excellent cutting horse. That just came natural to him.

In 1949 Marie bought Tom Moss's TWH. Tom had a ranch near Big Horn, Wyoming. Patty LaMarr, Black Beauty Allen, Ruby Jones, and others were added to Rickey's mare herd. The stallion, Buck LaMarr was also a big part of Marie's breeding program.

Marie's Tennessee Walkers were prominent in the Northwest and Canada. Buck LaMarr, Silvertip-Rickey, Lightfoot Rickey, Chief O' Chiefs, and Reveille Boy were all foundation sires.

Calvin Miller traded Marie a son of Roy Rogers Trigger Jr., Zephyr's Flash O Gold. One of the 2 fillies Marie traded to Calvin went on to be the dam of one of Gene Autrey's Champions. Red Cloud V was foaled in 1965.

The Canadian Walking Horse Registry has placed a number of Marie's foundation horses on their web site.

Circumstances change, not always for the better. Horse prices dropped drastically. Marie moved to Red Wing, Minnesota where she started working at the Seminary Home. It wasn't long before she began recycling on the side. Her Hauling & Recycling business grew and provided a living for her for close to 40 years.

I will use photos to tell the rest of her story. Marie passed away December 20, 2008.

Marie & Silvertip-Rickey 1950

An Immigrant, a Homesteader, and Sheep

Marie & Rishardson's Honey Chile
The Foal Is Chief O' Chiefs

Debs, Marie, Fay, Alice Grace 1945

Big Arm Place

Marie On Sunset 1941

Debs In 1939

Marie 85th Birthday

Lightfoot Rickey

Reveille Boy

Marie Poloson
on Sunset
Poloson Ranch
1938

Marie On Sunset 1939

Marie & Sunset 1939

Marie & Puppy By Carlin House

Marie's Class Lonepine Marie Is 3rd From Right

Lonepine School

Dan, Bert, Debs In Ranch House 1946

2nd Verse:
I knew that you'd won my heart, pard,
While riding the pine covered range.
Your eyes spoke of something, darling,
I hoped I would never see change.

3rd Verse:
The pale moon was high above us,
As slowly we two rode along.
I still can recall your yodel,
The lilt of your gay cowboy song.

4th Verse:
You said that my eyes were starlight,
My lips just as soft as the rain.
The scent of the rain in pine trees,
Will bring me those mem'ries again.

5th Verse:
But you rode away in the Autumn,
When range grass was growing so spare.
I stayed on the range so lonely,
Alone with my grief and despair.

Glass To Be Recycled

Marie On John Deere 1947

An Immigrant, a Homesteader, and Sheep

1000 Batteries Leave For Florida

Marie plowing snow with Bobcat

Recycling Drop

Recycling Building

An Immigrant, a Homesteader, and Sheep

On The Road In Virginia

Marie drove Semi for several years. She went to New York City, Texas, and all over much of the United States. She is pictured with co-driver, Fran.

Not only was Marie an expert on metals and recycling. She was a gifted writer and kept the Red Wing paper busy with her letters to the editor.

Marie knew all types of metal. She could weld, cut steel, dismantle engines, and appliances. Many tons of recycled metals went through Marie's shop.

Marie loved to read and she must have read several thousand books in her lifetime. She loved coffee and Perkins Restaurant.

Fred Poloson
age 12
1936

FRED HARRIS POLOSON

Fred's story has to be told mainly in photographs. I regret that I didn't set down with him and get his story. Fred passed away February 18, 2004.

He was an artist when it came to metal; it didn't matter the size from massive to miniature. Some of his work is displayed in the Museum Of America located near Polson, Montana.

Fred's early years of shoeing his father's pack horses, herding sheep, and working with the old Forge at the ranch were the foundation of amazing talent.

He was shoeing horses and mules for the Kootanai Forest Service when he was 17. He took over Bert's pack string in the St. Joe when Bert was drafted into the Army. In 1948 he and Bert went to work in Glacier Park. Fred blacksmithed and took the tough packing jobs. He could put 2-300 lbs. on a mule. In 1950 Fred went to work in Yellowstone Park blacksmithing.

Fred went to work on road jobs in Alaska in 1951. In 1955 and 1956 he took all his shop equipment to Noxon where he worked on the construction equipment that was used to build the dam. The rock work did a lot of damage to blades and buckets on the heavy equipment.

Fred Glacier Park 1949

Fred Glacier 1948

Hunting Camp Fred & John Cetescu

Fred On Casey Glacier Park

Alice On White "Ace" Gentle Gelding Fred &
Bert Gave Alice & Grace On Dusty

Fred By '47 International Essex, Montana

Bill Haynes & Fred Early '50's

Fred Driving Tanker from Great Falls to Spokane

Fred in Truck Alaska 1957

Fred Driving Uke (Eucalid) In Alaska

Fred & Ann Mid 1960's Poloson Ranch

Fred's Shop At Ranch Early 1940's

Fred 1954

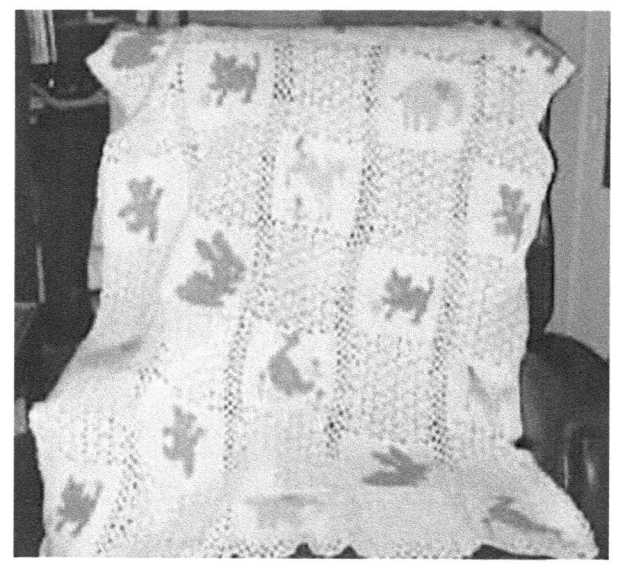

Ann's Crocheting & Knitting

Fred & Ann Columbia Falls, MT

Fred, Ann, Grace Plains, MT

Fred & Ann At A Blacksmith Gathering Lavina, MT

Fred & Ann & Lot's Of Fish

Fred designed & made All of These Shop Iron Working Machines

Fred's Field truck Doing Repairs for Logging Outfit

Fred's Sign Donated To Museum Of America Polson, MT

Fred's Hand Made Axes Displayed At the
Museum Of America Polson, MT

Museum Display Fred's Axes

Fred Designed & Made This Sign For Bert & Grace

Fred's Smokey

Fred With Ranch Pack Horses

Fred Going to the Sun Highway Glacier Park

Fred & George Wright (Rawhide)

Fred With Ranch Pack Horses Move Sheep Camp

Fred & Smokey

Fred 1947

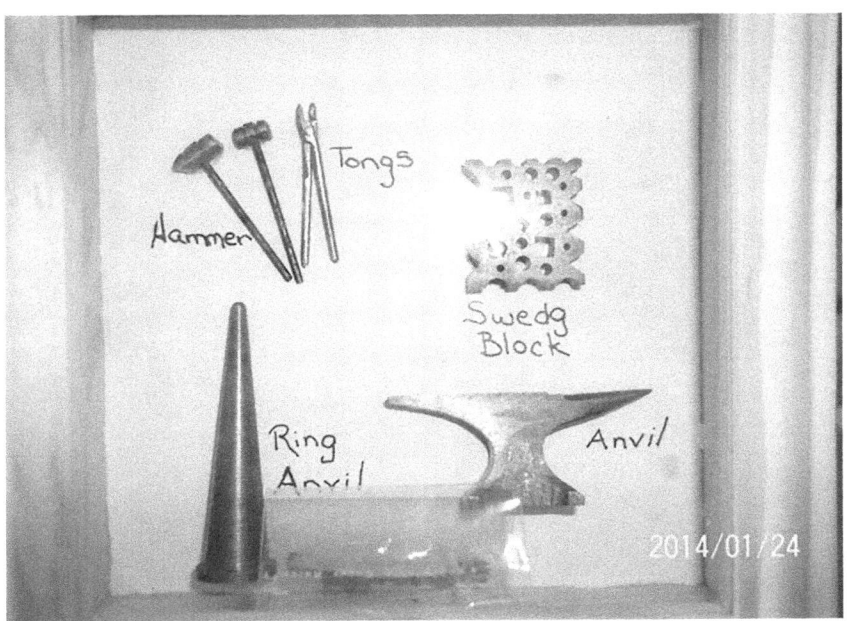

Miniature Tool Made By Fred & they All Work

Some Of Fred's Miniature Working Tools Displayed At His Funeral

Ann, was a wonderful help mate; she supported all that Fred did. And a better cook would be hard to find. She and Fred loved to camp and fish he was used to rugged camping and Ann never complained. A tarp thrown over a tree branch served as a roof many times. They traveled many miles as Fred worked various jobs on construction sites in Montana and Washington. They eventually made their home in Columbia Falls where Fred built a "state of the art" shop that could handle large equipment. He also created, from scratch, large pieces of equipment. Ann passed away in September of 2000.

Ann would camp with Fred until she was 91 or 92 years old. Fred would say, "Gotta Keep Her Going." They did get a camper for later years but still used the tarp over a limb shelter occasionally.

FAY'S STORY

I met Bill at a Polson rodeo. At that time I was rodeo secretary. Bill had a broken arm so he was judging; that was in nineteen forty nine, sixty one years ago! Bill was working for Bud Lake on his ranch near the Little Bitterroot River. I had no idea there was such a place; Sloan's Bridge? Never heard of it. I had hardly been to Ronan since we did ranch business in Hot Springs or Polson. On our first date we went to Polson and met some friends. We had dinner at the Ranch Night Club; it was a real popular place then, a place you went to when you were in Polson. Was I swept off my feet? Maybe. I knew so many of Bill's friends and also the people in Cutbank where he'd worked for several years. Bill had worked for Bud Lake for quite a while and I knew Bud and Mary Lake. We were married Dec. 15, 1951 at Bud Lake's home in Missoula. Just a few family, friends, and the minister were there. We went to the Grand Canyon for our honeymoon Bill came to Cutbank from Pine City, Minnesota when he was 12 years old. Getting to Cutbank was tough as he and an older boy had hopped a freight train. When it stopped along the way someone gave them a ring of bologna and a loaf of bread. The train started up too soon; the older boy made it back on with the bread but Bill dropped the ring of bologna as he ran and jumped onto the train. Bill's uncle had a ranch near Cutbank. At 12 Bill was already working for a living where ever there was a job, and they'd take him in and feed him. He was a hard worker and liked to work.

Bill started rodeoing when he was in the military. He and some of his buddies even put a rodeo on in Japan to the delight of the Japanese and the Army guys. When I met him he was still riding bulls and bareback horses. He also bull dogged and was good at it. Bill quit bareback horses and bulls soon after we were married. He started team roping and continued bull dogging; Bill was small but he could judge the steer's leg positions and be right on him.

An Immigrant, a Homesteader, and Sheep

We bought the ranch from Bud Lake in 1954; cattle, ranch, and all. It was a real nice place except for the wind and rattlesnakes. That wind seemed like it could blow across the river, hit the mountain, and bounce back. There was a big snake den up on the hillside. We had it dynamited and we even poured gas all over it trying to burn them out; we never did get rid of the snakes. A couple of foals were bitten. Foals are so curious and would put their nose right down to check out the snake. Both recovered.

There were bear back of our place. They liked the chokecherries. The Moss boys roped a bear back there. I think they choked him down so they could get the rope off; his hind feet were thrashing all the time. The Moss boys were tough kids.

I had Arabians before we were married. Bill was a quarter horse man so we sold the Arabs and went into quarter horses. I got serious about barrel racing after we bought Jule Bar in the mid 50's. I'd ride Jule Bar around the barrels when I'd ride out to the mail box and on the way back we'd trot around the barrels, so he learned the pattern well. I had started barrel racing with a sorrel Thoroughbred, Arrow. Lila Mae Stewart helped train me and the horse.

Bill ran horses for canner buyer, Sicard, who had bought about fifty head from the prison ranch. The big sorrel Thoroughbred horse didn't fit that bunch; he was a good looking horse. Each horse had to be bid on; they wouldn't allow a buyer to bid on the entire bunch. A guy put a bid in on a group but auctioneer wouldn't accept the bid. Sicard bought another sorrel, Gold Creek, a real pretty red sorrel with three stock- ings, a star, and strip. He was ready to run if anyone came riding towards him; he was pretty but wild. One day Bert came riding by on Gold Creek; he was a good, smooth traveler. Bert said "some people have quantity but I have quality." Gold Creek was just plum wild but he never did buck. Where Gold Creek or Arrow came from no one knows; they weren't branded. The rest of the prison bunch were work horse types made up of blacks and browns. Bert could even shoot off of Gold Creek and he'd never move a muscle.

Another time we rounded up a bunch of horses and ran them down to a lane. I had them in a fence corner, or so I thought. When they came towards me they split up and they were gone. I was riding

Night who was an excellent saddle horse. They finally shot those horses because they could never catch them.

We trained Arrow to ride; he was half way broke when we got him. Lila Mae started him on barrels; she and I were traveling to rodeos together then. We went to the finals in White Sulphur in September. It rained for three days; there was no place to stay so we stayed in the horse trailer. We did have sleeping bags with us. The next morning snow was on the ground. We both ran barrels; that was the last time I used Arrow. We sold him to a girl for High School rodeo.

Jule Bar liked barrel racing; he was always calm and never got excited; he would dance a bit but he was never out of control. If I didn't get after him he'd go to sleep. Jumpy Jule was pretty much like his Dad. Breese was the only excitable horse I had. He could out run anything I'd ever been on; his father was Top Breese by Top Deck; he was always rearing to go; his dam was a Jule Bar mare. Breese was an easy horse to handle. Our little neighbor boy ran barrels on him; that's when I decided to run him on barrels. I had never run barrels with him but he took to it right at the start. I won three jackpots in a row. I was going to Deer Lodge next. When the horses came up the lane I opened the gate so they could come into the corral. Breese was cut severely clear to his tendon with the skin stripped all the way to the bone. Breese spent three months with the vet. Later on I rode him a few times once over on the Moss' place. It took three years for the hide to grow back and he wasn't lame at all. Breeze was 26 when he died.

We usually hired somebody to put up our hay; we did put it up with the team but it got to be too much work. Carrol Hopkins hayed for us for a long time. We kept about 12 brood mares and bought, trained, and sold horses. Plus calving and all the work that goes with cattle. After we lost Jule Bar in the Missoula Fair fire, August of 1967, Bill found a stallion in Denver; we didn't like him that well.

Next, we went to Idaho and bought a stallion; he had a nice build but he was so clumsy; he would get his feet tangled up. We sold him to a guy from Kalispell; the horse didn't have to turn when roping calves so he did okay. We went to Oklahoma City and bought Triple Coen by Lightening Bar. We looked at a horse over at Bozeman too but we never really found anything that could match Jule Bar.

The ranch had a small house on it. We built onto it after we bought the ranch in 1954. We sold the ranch in 1972 and moved to this 80 acre place near Ronan. Bill passed away in 1975. After Bill died I saw where Mark Parker had a colt; he wanted ten thousand for him. Mark sent me photos and his pedigree. He was a good stallion and crossed so well on Jule Bar mares. I called the stallion "Parker" after his breeder. I continued with the horses and started teaching barrel racing. After the arena was built I hosted team ropings, jumping, and other horse activities, and I have continued to do this into 2014, and I hope I can do so for several more years. I have continued to ride and I'm looking for another saddle horse now (spring of 2014). I was 88 January 4th.

I sold the last of our mares to Kelly & Tracy in Canada. They had taken a vacation which included a trip to the ranch where First Down Dash was. Tracy had her picture taken with her hand on him. One of those mares we sold is now 31 years old. We called her the wild mare; she'd never been haltered, vaccinated, or anything but she out lived them all. She had colts every year. The old mare is a babysitter for the weanlings now. Tracy is running a colt out of that old mare. Their QH, Six Pack Of Corona, had won his last five races. Some guys in Arizona said "they don't have horses in Canada" but they do! Corona goes back to Easy Jet.

Fay Haynes on Cool Hand Luke

Fay & Gold Creek

Fay & Lucille Roullier

An Immigrant, a Homesteader, and Sheep

Kevin Bach on Jule Bar
Great Aunt Fay Haynes on lead
1960

Fay & Bert
Glacier Park

Fay & Jule Bar Winning The Montana Quarter Horse Association Barrel Racing Championship 1965

Mr. & Mrs. Bill Haynes Ready to Leave For Their Honeymoon In The Grand Canyon

Bill Haynes on Jule Bar Branding At Meltons

An Immigrant, a Homesteader, and Sheep

Bill Haynes In Japan About 1945

Fay Poloson Haynes, Dan Poloson, Bill Haynes – 1960

Bill & Fay Haynes Big Bend Ranch House

Fay Poloson 1949
Age 23
on Night best horse
she ever owned

Night "One of the Best"

    One of the best times I remember was trailing Jake Johnson's 48 head of bucking horses from Phillipsburg, MT to Hamilton, MT. It was 62 miles by way of Skalkaho Pass. This was in about 1949. Marilyn Barnes Miller and I rode good horses. I was riding Night; he was so smooth when he hit a rack, and he had a lot of stamina. The horses had just been bucked at Phillipsburg. Next was the Hamilton rodeo. We each had toast and coffee before we left and we didn't eat again until we got to Hamilton! We had left Phillipsburg at 10 AM and arrived in hamilton by 9 that evening.

    That trip was the most fun ever! We stopped at the beautiful Skalkaho Falls. The country around us was breath taking. Some people from British Columbia stopped to visit us at the Falls; they admired our horses.

I did spend a lot of weekends in Glacier Park when Bert & Fred were there. I usually rode a Park horse.

In my lifetime I have ridden some mighty fine horses and covered beautiful country. My years with Bill were busy and happy. We enjoyed so many things together; most of it involved work but it was good.

Jule Bar and Night are my favorites but it is hard to judge so many good horses.

Courtesy of the Valley Journal Ronan, MT
And The Quarter Horse Journal

An Immigrant, a Homesteader, and Sheep

Fay-Trophies

Fay Haynes inducted into Montana Cowboy Hall of Fame

Courtesy Of The Valley Journal Ronan, MT

Fay Haynes

from page 18

round up stallions on Wildhorse Island so Doc Burnett could geld them.

To manage the growing herd, one time she helped roundup 49 of the 94 horses on the island and transport them on a flat barge across the choppy water to Elmo. Fay recalled her husband keeping a pocketknife razor sharp, so he could cut the horses loose in the event the barge started to sink. Luckily the barge stayed above water. Once they reached Elmo, the healthy stock was carted to Missoula and sold.

In 1973, the couple bought acreage west of Pablo and built their home together. Bill passed away just two years later, and Haynes never remarried.

Through the years Fay has taught numerous young girls to barrel race, and trained their horses as well. Several have gone on to win substantial awards. And the ropers still come to her home to practice twice a week.

Haynes never considered a different lifestyle, she said, although the community has changed dramatically in her time.

Following her induction to Montana's Cowboy Hall of Fame, Haynes reflected on her life and accomplishments.

"It's been a long ride, but this was what I was meant to do," she said.

An Immigrant, a Homesteader, and Sheep

Courtesy Of The Valley Journal Ronan, MT

Rodeo Star

Top Hand Continued: Trophy Won By Jule Bar

WILD HORSE ISLAND ROUNDUP

Up in northwestern Montana in *big sky country*, lies a clear, beautiful lake known as Flathead, named for the Flathead Indian tribe. And about 28 miles long and 15 miles wide, this lake has furnished entertainment for tourists from far and wide with its boating, water skiing, and fishing; and the beauty along its shore lines has been the subject of photography and enjoyment by people from all walks of life.

This area is also well-known for its farms, ranches, friendly towns, and the delicious sweet cherries grown so abundantly along the lake's shores.

Another attraction of the Flathead Lake is Wild Horse Island, situated in the southwestern part of the lake, about a mile offshore at the closest point. Not too much is known of the history of the island except by the oldtimers and people living in the area. However, it is of interest to passers-by who marvel at this unusual and picturesque island in what is known as Montana's *paradise.*

At one time there were many homesteads on the island, which has about 3,00 acres. When the country was opened to homesteading in 1910, the island was included, and among the first homesteaders were L.E. Thurber, Roy Torkinson, a Mr. Norberg, Mr. Powers, and the famous German photographer, Herman Schnitzmeyer.

In 1915, the government sold land in the lake area as villa sites, and Col. A.A. White of St. Paul purchased several sites on Wild Horse Island.

Judge Padbury and Mr. Penwell owned land on the island, as well as did the state university and the Indian Department. Penwell operated Hiawatha Lodge on the east end for some time, and ran a bunch of horses on the island.

On the west shore of the Lake near Rollins was the Clatterbuck Guest Ranch, owned and operated by Mr. and Mrs. Guy Clatterbuck and son, Ted, and a very popular resort at the time. It was to Clatterbucks that Dr. J.C. Burnett and his wife came from New York to spend their vacations during World War II. Dr. Burnett was a retired osteopath, and his wife was an heiress to a roller bearing corporation. Doc, as he was called, became interested in the island, and decided he would own his unique land. Money was of no concern to the Burnetts, but the big job would be to locate the owners and heirs of the island. So they hired A.L. (Lloyd) Helmer of Polson and set out to gather the necessary information. After a year's travel and investigation, the papers were finally in order; Doc was able to buy every foot of the island, and only then would be put his money down.

This was a great new undertaking for Doc, and he spent considerable time on the island. Mrs. Burnett was an elderly lady, and the wild west held little appeal to her, so she spent but one summer there.

Doc had hired Guy Clatterbuck as superintendent of the island. Guy was a well-known and popular cowboy in the country. And so began the years of enjoyment (and hard work) that went with Wild Horse Island. Many trips back and forth in a boat were sometimes pleasant, sometimes highly dangerous, because Flathead Lake in a storm can be mighty wild.

The first thing done was to hire two more cowboys, Bud Lake and Bob Gray, and clear all the horses from the island. A few of these horses Ted Clutterbuck broke, and the rest were sold. Then Doc proceeded to buy mares from here and there over the country and move them to the island by barge, to be turned loose on the range. He bought a very classic purebred Arabian stallion in Arizona and turned him loose with the mares. This horse was used to being pampered, and his life was difficult those first few years as a range horse, especially in winter.

His next step was to buy Riskulus, a Thoroughbred stallion in Kentucky, for $33,000. Riskulus was sired by Stimulus, by Ultimus, and had an enviable record on the track at the time. From 1933 through 1936 he won $32,000 on the race track, a lot of money in those days of small purses. He won at many of the best tracks, and set a track record at Santa Anita for the mile and an eighth as a four-year-old.

Riskulus was cared for in his own pen and barn on the island, but was bred to only a few mares. He was shipped back to Kentucky for the winter, and the following spring Doc shipped him back to Montana and gave him to Bud Lake. Doc had almost lost interest in the horses by that time, and his interest in the island was also fast waning. Other businesses and investments in all parts of the world claimed his attention.

The deer were plentiful on Wild Horse Island, and every fall about hunting season they would swim from shore to Cromwell, a small island between shore and Wild Horse, and then on to the main island. Many times in the fall over 400 deer would roam the island. Then mountain sheep, two ewes and a ram, were turned loose on the island, to begin what would amount to well over 100 sheep in a fairly short time. This was ideal country for the sheep — dry, rough, and with timbered draws to hide in.

An Immigrant, a Homesteader, and Sheep

An Immigrant, a Homesteader, and Sheep

Doc loved animals, and the deer, mountain sheep, and wild horses on the island were a great source of entertainment for him. Guy had found him a good saddle horse, a big sorrel from the New Lynch ranch at Plains, half-Thoroughbred and half-Percheron. Doc and his outfit weighed around 275 pounds, so it took more than just an average horse to carry him over that rough country. He was fond of Chief, though he rode the horse hard when he did ride him. Riding a form-fitting saddle, he loved to chase horses with the cowboys. He would ride up high on one of the ridges, throw old Chief his head, and go whooping and yelling down the sidehill, as they said, "like a pebble down a well." It would chill you, visioning the horse falling and the pair of them rolling clear to the lake! Fortunately Chief was extra good on his feet.

Doc was a kind-hearted, generous, and friendly man, and this big new, open country was to his liking at the time, and perhaps it gave him some of the most fun he had in his life.

A deer that stayed around the main house was thought to be a pet of the Penwell children. She gathered all her friends and relatives, and they moved in to eat the saddle horses' hay and grain. Every time the horses were fed, Dinah and her pals were right there for their share.

Doc decided he should have a horse breaker on the island, so Guy hired Hill Haynes who was rodeoing at the time, and the big chore began. Doc wanted the mares broke, and although most of them were never touched again, Bill broke those old wild, snakes mares to ride. That was the summer Mrs. Burnett was on the island, and she and Doc spent long hours in the jeep up at the horse corrals watching Bill work with the horses. It was ll fun to Doc, and many times he would follow Bill along the lakeshore or sidehills in his jeep, banging on the sides and whooping to stampeded the horse. This didn't go over so well with Bill at first, but he finally realized it was the way Doc wanted it, and after all, he was paying the bills and they were his horses. So let him have his fun! There was also a mule on the island, and Doc insisted on Bill riding it for the amusement of his friends. Finally the mule quit bucking which ended that.

Doc liked to kiss his horses on the nose, and many times barley escaped a hoof on his chin. He wanted to ride all the horses, too; and finally there was one little bay mare that got pretty gentle, so one day Doc rode her out to help gather horses. They came for the corrals on a run as usual, this time Doc right in their midst. The first thing Bill knew, Doc was on his back on the ground, a foot hung in his stirrup. Luckily the little are stood while Bill quietly took Doc loose. The big man was trying to run his horse into the corral, set her up, and step off "like you cowboys do."

The horses were mainly sorrels with white markings, with almost all the young ones at least half-Arabian. The colts were gelding in the fall with Bill doing the veterinarian chores. Many a roundup was held with Guy, Bill, and me doing most of the riding. Sometimes horses from the island were used, but mainly special horses were brought from shore by barge.

It took a good horse to travel this country and successfully gather the stock that had run wild all their lives, the case with most of them. The terrain was rough, steep, and rocky; the horses were wily, smart, tough and used to the country.

Some favorite horses on these island roundups were Bill's Iron Horse, a brown Thoroughbred that only knew the word *go;* Night, a black horse I usually rode was a Thoroughbred-Morgan-Arabian cross, not a very pretty horse, but what a horse runner — he loved it and he seemed to know just what those horses were going to do all the time; Red, a son of Riskulus owned by Guy, a big, beautiful sorrel horse that proved himself a top horse on the island; and Eagle, a cream-colored horse raised by us, just a young horse but tough and willing. Generally this work was too hard for an unseasoned horse so mainly the older, tough using horses were taken to the island. Sand and Chief, two of the island horses were sometimes used, as well as a few of the gentler ones Bill had broke to ride, if extra riders were on hand.

In 1954, there were over 100 range horses on the island, and Doc decided to sell half of them. At one time he planned to ship them to New York but decided this would be impractical. He sent word to Guy, telling him which horses he wanted saved, and the roundup began that fall. A crew built corrals, fences, and a wing to the shoreline where the horses were to be loaded on a barge.

An Immigrant, a Homesteader, and Sheep

Riding on this las troundup were Guy Clatterbuck and Bill and myself. Special care was to be given to get every horse in the corrals this time, and the best saddle horses were taken to the isalnd. Hodge's Barge from Polson was hired, and it was a real thrill, riding form Polson to the island, about a three-hour trip along the quiet lake. High sides had been built on the big flat bed of the barge which was complete with living quarters.

This was truly an unforgettable experience, gathering the horses, cutting them out, turning those back on the island that were to stay, and loading the rest on the barge — 49 head of them, and three saddle horses. The wild ones were almost frightened to death, but rode safely to shore near Elmo, where they were corralled and loaded on trucks to go to Missoula and the sale ring.

In the late winter of 1956, reports were made to the humane society that the horses were going hungry on the island, that the snow was too deep, and the grass was gone. Contact was made with Doc, who ordered baled hay flow from Polson to the island. In the opinion of the ranchers in the country, this was very well done, except for one thing; when a horse is eating hay, he must have water. With only grass to eat, snow will replace water. But the horses filled up on fresh, green hay, and could get no water since the lake was frozen over. Consequently most of them died of impaction and this good deed by the humane society backfired. When the chinooks took the snow a while later, a tragic sight greeted the eyes of visitors to the island. There were four horses and a mule living, and apparently in good shape. Perhaps the others, or most of them, would have survived if left to Nature; who knows?

So the beautiful sorrel horses would run down the ridges and canyons no more, and the glory of Wild Horse Island was gone forever.

Doc came no more. His was preceded him in death, and when Doc passed a few years later, the island was put up for sale. But we who rode there can still vision those beautiful horses running wild and free, and remember all the good times we had on the roundups — deer, sheep, and horses,, all in a band — where else on earth is there such a setting as this?

ALBERT RAYMOND POLOSON

When I was 15 I went to Arizona and worked for a farmer hilling cantaloupe fields, and doing other jobs with his caterpillar. I came back to the ranch and helped feed the sheep and cattle. Jake Johnson needed a guy to haul bucking horses and bulls so I did that for a while.

Arvid Kopp was packing in the St. Joe country of Idaho. He talked me into going to work over there and taking his job. I was 17 years old that year, 1945. A man named Joe Schultz was quite a fisherman. He kept them in the snow. Every time I rode over to see him he'd fry some fish.

During the 50's I worked at several different jobs and continued helping at the ranch. I had a job running shovel near Perma for Miller & Stone Construction. Then I ran scraper when Highway 93, west of Polson, was under construction. It was my job to make the "first cut off the hill" as they built the road. That was a terrible, dusty job. They didn't have water trucks which would have kept that dust down. The contractor was from Great Falls. When he brought the rest of his crew over and laid me off I was glad to go.

I went to work up the North Fork of the Flathead River running scraper. That was wet country so the dust wasn't too bad.

Heavy Equipment contractors needed experienced hands. The Noxon Dam was being built and I got on there running shovel at the rock quarry for Peter Kiewit Construction.

Through most of the 1960's I had my own trucks and some heavy equipment. I started hauling silver ore from Battle Butte, north of Niarada, to the smelter in Anaconda. During this time I started a logging business too. I had close to a dozen employees; sawyers, loaders, and drivers. We took 18 million board feet out on one sale which was located in the back country near the east shore of Flathead Lake. Those logs all went to Plum Creek Mill at Pablo, Montana.

I had bought a back hoe so made a nice fish pond on the Vander Ende Homestead Dad had bought. It came with the ranch purchase in 1929. I made some more lakes for area farmers.

Betty & I had divorced in 1971. I'd bought the place near Polson that year. Grace and I were married in Mullen, Idaho July 6, 1972. It was a "spur of the moment" wedding since we had both trucks and were picking up a load in Spokane. All of our paperwork was done so we stopped in Mullen on our way back. Grace had 2 daughters, Susan and Verna, and Betty and I had Jeanne & Russell. Jeanne had graduated High School and was living in Great Falls. Russell finished his last year of high school in Polson. Susan was 18 & Verna 17 when we were married.

This place was barren without any trees when we bought it. We built a big machine shop right away. Today it has so many trees that I have to keep thinning our little forest.

During the 1960's I had started buying, repairing, and selling heavy equipment. After Grace & I were married we traveled all over to auctions getting some really good buys. We took a Ferry to Vancouver Island where we bought some heavy equipment from a friend. Most of these trips were to Edmonton and Calgary, Alberta but we did go as far as North Carolina. Truckers from that area could haul a lot cheaper than we could so we arranged for them to haul if we had something coming in from the SE.

We bought a Mack truck out of California in 1973. That's the last new one we bought. We had 3 Macks and sold all but the one we bought in 1973. That one was sold when we retired.

During the 70's we had the fire contract for the tribe. We'd bought a TD-30 Cat; it hadn't gotten here so I called Charlie Crane and asked him, "When will that cat get here?" Fire season was here and no cat. Finally, the trucker showed up. I asked him, "When did you leave Kansas?" He replied, "When did Charlie tell you I left?" We had several pieces of heavy equipment out on different fires. We had a radio that was connected to Tribal Headquarters at Pablo.

Grace went with me to auctions most of the time. Travel got so tiring that I decided to get a Pilot's License. I was able to start flying to auctions in 1976. Grace learned to fly and she had earned

2 licenses by 1977; 1 for the land plane and 1 for the sea plane. We bought our first float plane November of 1979 in New York. We sold that in November of 1981. We still have the float plane we bought in 1982. We bought a Cessna land plane in 1982 and used that to fly to auctions. That saved so much time.

We used the float plane to fly up into the Yukon and Northwest Territories. Some areas were in British Columbia and some were in Alberta. We crossed the Arctic Circle a couple of times. We usually camped out but we did stay in Yellowknife for 3 days. That's been over 30 years ago!

We saw bear, moose, deer, and caribou. There were some Grizzlies. Once we'd camped right on a bear trail. Grace heard "clicking" sounds as the little bear came up the trail. He just went around us and then went on up the hill. Another time we'd camped by a creek; that bear came closer to camp but he crossed the creek to get to better going.

I had grown up spending my summers in mountain sheep camps, and Grace had grown up near Great Falls with parents who loved the outdoors and hunting, so these trips to the North Country were very special for us.

Grace:

I became a teacher. I spent some time in Yellowstone Park then got a job teaching 3 children in Wisdom, Montana in an area known as the Big Hole Country. These children were in the 1st, 3rd, and 8th grades. That winter it got down to 51 below zero! I chopped wood and built the fire so the room would warm up by the time the children arrived. They brought their own water. The snow got so deep school was cancelled for several months. I stayed with a family that let me use their pickup or a saddle horse so I could get to the school. I enjoyed fishing and hunting while I was there.

My next job was in Divide, Montana where I taught the first 3 grades. Then I took a job in a one room school near Somers teaching grades 1-8. I bought a home in Somers and taught there for 7 years. Susan was born in 1953 and Verna in 1954. Both while I taught in Somers.

Before I had any children I had lived in Alaska where my husband followed the gold mines. I was in Alaska for 7 months then took a teaching job at Battle Butte for 1 term. then I moved back to Somers where I taught. The girls and I went to Alaska again to the same place I'd been years before, and to the same trailer. I home schooled Verna and Susan. They were in the 1st and 3rd grade. On our way to the gold mines I shot 3 caribou. They were our meat for the winter. We hunted and fished a lot while we were there.

I resumed teaching in Somers when we came back to Montana. When the job came up at the isolated Battle Butte one room school NW of Niarada, Montana I decided to buy a trailer house because of the distance from Somers. I taught grades 1-8 for 3 years. I just loved that place and the children were so well behaved. They were ages 6 through 13. I had a girl named Judy in the 3rd grade. She told me then that she was going to marry a boy named Lee, and she sure enough did! They live on the Borden place near Niarada.

I met Bert when he was hauling ore from the Battle Butte mine. It was "love at first sight." After we were married I became very involved in our business. November 23, 1977 was a special day for me; that is when I received my pilot certificates for private and sea plane licenses.

During our years at our Polson place I have planted trees and flowers. Our place is so different from the barren surroundings we had in 1972. I accompany Bert when he flies but at age 88 (2014) I no longer pilot our planes.

Bert & Grace 1973 At New Place Not One Tree On The Place 185 Skywagon Float Plane

An Immigrant, a Homesteader, and Sheep

1982 Cadillac They Still Drive, Grace, Bert, & Their Float Plane

Moving Float Plane to the River

Float Plane At Polson, Montana Marina

Loading Float Plane to Go To Vancouver, Bc

Float Plane at Polson Airport

Bert's Crane At Dan Poloson Ranch Earl 1960's

Bert's Drag Line Making A Lake For A Polson Area Farmer

Sixty Caterpillar

One Of Three Mack Trucks Bert & Grace Hauled Equipment With

Bert on Buffalo Poloson Ranch Mid 1940's

Bert Moving Plywood & Ties with Mule String Glacier Park 1949

Bert & Brown Horse 1949

Bert Training A Mule To Pack

Bert & Chief With Pack Mules Glacier Park 1949

Bert McDonald Pass, Montana 1947

Don Barnum & Bert Glacier Park 1948

An Immigrant, a Homesteader, and Sheep

Bert With Mule String Glacier Park

Bert's Saddle Horse & Mule String Glacier Park 1948

Dan Poloson At Fay & Bill's 1968

Poloson Family 1972 Bill Haynes, Fay, Bert, Grace, Fred, Ann, Dan

Dan And His Cat 1973

Chopping Hay for the Ewes

Ewes & Lambs

An Immigrant, a Homesteader, and Sheep

Hay Sling Unloading Hay At Poloson Ranch Mid 1940's

*Pal At Poloson Ranch Mail Box 4 Miles From Ranch House
Mae Poloson's Bar MP and Fay's Lazy Anchor Brands*

Romanian Friend With Fay & Dan In Romania 1972

Dan With Family Members In Romania

*1972 Photos Taken In Porumbacu, Romania,
Dan Poloson's Birth Place*

*Aurelia & Magdalena Visit America.
Photo Taken At Bert & Grace Poloson's
In 1975 Dan Made Their Trip Possible*

Bert Poloson 87 Years Old Removing Tree 2013

Fay & Dan In Bucharest, Romania 1972

Bringing The Tree Down

MAE POLOSON POEMS RETYPED BY JEANNE POLOSON BRONEC

COYOTE'S SERENADE

By Mae Poloson

Chorus:
Yippee, yippee, you ooo,
Sounds the coyote's tune,
Yippy-yippy-you ooo,
Sung to the risin' moon,
All of the joys I'm missin',
All of the plans we made,
Come to my mind as I listen
To the coyote's serenade.

If you were here tonight, dear,
Loneliness would take wings;
If I could hold you tight, dear,
While the coyote sings,
If I had wealth and power,
These I would gladly trade
To listen with you for an hour
To the coyote's serenade.

Sweetheart, the day is over,
I sit and think of you
While the coyote, that sly rover,
Sends out his yippy-yoo.
Once I loved to listen
For you were by my side,
And we watched the moonlight glisten
On the prairie far and wide.
Now there's no denyin'
Since we are far apart,
I hear in the coyote's cryin'
The call of a lonely heart.

Moonstruck

By Mae Poloson

Last night you said "I love you", and
I never thought to doubt it;
This morning I've been thinking and
Wondering about it.
Did you say "I love you"
Just to be romantic?
I've been asking, wondering,
'Til I'm almost frantic.
Did the sly moon trap you with her
And well-known magic?
I must know the answer
Even tho' it's tragic.

When October Turns the Maple Leaves to Gold

By Mae Poloson

Thru the meadows sweet with hay
Strolled a youth and maid one day,
And they spoke about their love as sweethearts will.
As the sun sank in the West
There they paused awhile to rest,
'Neath a maple tree that stands beside a rill.
And he said 'Just one more day,
Then I'm going far away
And the parting fills my hears with grief untold.
Will you promise to be true
Until I come back to you,
When October turns the maple leaves to gold?

Chorus:
When October turns the maple leaves to gold,
I'll retell the sweetest story ever told.
For I'm coming back to you,
And we'll pledge our love anew,
When October turns the maple leaves to gold.

From a city far away
Came a message, sad, one day,
For it said the one she loved was in his grave.
Soon the broken-hearted maid
'Neath the maple tree was laid,
In a grave where golden branches gently wave.
But the wise old peoples say

On a a hazy, Autumn day,
That the sweethearts come as in the long ago,
And they say that hand in hand
'Neath the maple tree they stand,
While a soft wind seems to murmur sweet and low:
(Repeat Chorus)

Sunset Light

By Mae Poloson

Now the sunset light is falling
On the shrine beside the sea,
From the mosque the deep-toned mullah
Unto prayer is calling me.

Oh, Allah, blessed Allah,
Fain I'd worship at the shrine,
But a tent beneath a palm tree
Calls this wayward heart of mine.

So softly on the temple
Falls the light from western skies,
 But the glow that lights my pathway
Is the light of laughing eyes.

Now the sunset light has faded
From the shrine beside the sea,
As a weary, heartsore pilgrim,
Allah, turns at last, to thee.

As the sunlight from the temple,
So the light of laughing eyes,
Faded from my life's horizon
Leaving only darkened skies.

There's not much doing in Rattlesnake Gulch,
Where the rattlers bask in the garden mulch;
So I kill time just a-watchin' my dog
Solemnly driving a small green frog.

Grace E Larson

Pup, don't you think that you have descended
To a lower status than Nature intended!
Your ma would be shocked, the poor little bitch,
Shocked or grieved, I don't know which,

To know that she had raised a son or daughter,
Whose only task is to drive frogs to water.
(Pup to writer)
(And your ma might be grieved, you lazy oaf,
To know that you only sit and loaf.)

I Believe

By Mae Poloson

I believe that man can save
The world from the state it's in,
That black shades slowly thru gray to white,
 And sin is not always sin.

I believe there are righteous ways
That the old saints never trod,
I believe that each soul must find
Its own lone way to God.

I believe there are many ways
Of looking at many things;
I have seen crows in the sunset light,
Flying on silver wings.

Compensation

By Mae Poloson

The chill winds, blowing across my brow,
Scatter the tears I've shed;
Life cannot harm me further now,
I have buried my dead.

For Love is dead, but Faith died first,
And Love, seeing Faith depart,
Withered and died like a thing accurst,
Or struck by a fiery dart.

So I buried them both, but could not leave
Their grave unmarked, alone,
I hardened my heart lest I stay to grieve,
And left it there for a stone.

I see but a lonely road ahead,
But I'm not afraid of Life;
The strength I found to bury my dead
Will take me through storm or strife

And disappointment can never break
A heart that's already dead,
So it does not matter which way I take,
Or what I shall find ahead.

This 'N' That

By Mae Poloson

Lay in more grub for the new week-ends,
For the airplane's with us now.
We can all expect that our distant friends
Will be dropping DOWN for chow.

CAMPFIRE REVERIE

By Mae Poloson

The campfire flickers and slowly dies,
Far overhead a nighthawk cries,
A coyote sings his "Yip, Yip, Yoo,"
And a lone owl questions, "Who, Who?"
Questions and waits, but no voice replys,
While a slim, new moon in the Western skies,
Sinks like a lovely, golden ship.
Wrecked and sunk on her maiden trip.
And I ask as I gaze on that starry sea,
Will my ship of dreams come back to me?
Not a voice replies to me or the owl,
But away in the West, the coyotes howl,
Howl like demons, dancing with glee,
On my ship of dreams that was lost at sea.
Each goodbye is a little death,
So sharp a stab of pain.
Oh, please look back and smile at me,
And I shall live again.

Prairies at Midnight

By Mae Poloson

Sadly I wait on the prairie,
Since you have gone away.
 Lonely I am, and weary
Missing you night and day.
Here, where I kissed you, knowing
We two were doomed to part,
While the campfire faintly glowing
Died like the hope in my heart.
The prairies at midnight are whispering your name,
The little stream murmurs it too,
The hills in the distance are still the same,
The only thing missing is you.
The prairies are listening, the silent hills wait,
As I am still waiting here too,
For the one precious gift I am asking of fate,
Is to share these wide prairies with you.

By Mae Poloson

I never knew what love was like,
Nor did I greatly care,
Until I walked into a room
And saw you standing there.
And then I knew the singing birds
Were made to sing of love,
And I knew too, that sweethearts true,
Own all the stars above.
I never knew that hearts could break,
And life could still go on,
Until I sought for you one day
And knew that you were gone.

And then I knew my lonely heart
Could ne'er again forget,
And life, for me, would always be
One long and vain regret.
But if someday I see your face,
Among the hurrying throng,
My heart once more will beat in time,
With every bluebird's song.
Once more I'll see the sunlight clear,
For me the stars will shine,
And each new day, I'll go my way,
Content, for you are mine.

BY MAY POLOSON

I am sitting alone here tonight on the strand,
While the moon sheds its light on the sea;
I remember a time in m y own happy land
When you promised that you'd wait for me.
But the days have gone by and I've wandered afar,
From my home and all this I hold dear.
Still the memory shines like a bright guiding star,
As the time of reunion draws near.
And I know you'll be true to the promises giv'n,
In the days when the world all seemed fair,
And I long for my home as a saint longs for heaven,
For I know you are waiting for me.
Still I sit here tonight all alone on the shore,
While the moon paints a silvery sea,
And I dream I am back in my own land once more,
Where I find you still waiting for me.

Kiss it and Make It Well

By Mae Poloson

Mother, I hurt my knee today,
On a sharp stone I fell,
Leaving a hurt that will not go away,
Kiss it and make it well.
Back in the days of long ago,
Oh what a comfort it was to know
Mother could cure all my young heart's woe,
Kiss it and make it well.

Mother, I broke my heart one day,
Deeply in love I fell,
Leaving an ache that will not go away,
Kiss it and make it well.
Take me again to your gentle heart,
Bid this sharp pain from my life depart,
Comfort me with your healing art,
Kiss it and make it well.

"Mother Knows Best"

The brown hen led the duckling so proudly from the nest,
And straightway tried to teach them that Mother knows what's best.
But each little yellow puff-ball went merrily down the lane To splash in the shining puddles left by the warm spring rain.

And all the brown hen's clucking checked not their duckish zest;;
'Twas plain she'd never teach them that Mother knows what's best. As the housewife stood and listened to the worried, clucking hen, She thought of other years gone by, the boys were little then.

Now they are grown and scattered through North, South, East and West,
Because she could not teach them that Mother knows what's best.
And her husband, smiling gently, said, "Ma, I'll bet ten bucks
You know just how that brown hen feels . . . our family too, were ducks!"

"Isolationist"

By Mae Poloson

I heard this story long years ago when I was a credulous lad.
If it had a moral, I never knew, nor did I care if it had.
There lived a man who was no man's friend, and he had no friends of his own
He asked no help and he offered none, and People left him alone.
When this man died and went to Hell, as usual, he traveled alone;
The Devil gave him some coals and said, "Go start a Hell of your own".

"To Kathie"

By Mae Poloson

Kathie, you are a shadow cool, where a weary one finds rest,
Rest for even the errant fool, home from his fruitless quest.
Kathie, you are a sparkling well to quench a bitter thirst,
To wash from memory the hell of life in a land accursed.

All of these things and many more, Kathie, you are to me;
Source of the joys I've known before, hope of the things to be.
Kathie, you are the greatest gift that life to me has given;
You are the reason that I lift grateful eyes to Heaven.

I had my family tree looked up, and now I don't deny it; It cost a lot to look it up, but more to keep it quiet!

LOST FAITH

There grows a plant upon this hill,
That's tall and stately when it's still,
But when the wind its seed pods shake
It sounds quite like a rattlesnake.

Once I believed, in early youth,
That Nature held the key to truth,
But where find Truth beneath the sky,
When e'en a pale, dead plant can lie?

Dry Lander

Down on the irrigated ranches,
Robins are counted a sign of Spring.
There by the streams, in the willow branches,
Cheery and sweet the bird-notes ring.
Here, in the sagebrush is no singing,
Still, Spring cannot be far away'
Soon it will come, its brief flowers bringing,
I heard a rattlesnake today!

LITTLE JOYS

The little joys are mine today,
The joy of birds that sing,
The sheen of sunshine flashing clear,
Upon a blue bird's wing.
The sound of bees on apple boughs,
Their soft and vibrant hum,
The little joys are mine today,
The great ones may not come.

****

Oh, I think of you dear, in the evening,
I dream of you still, in the night; And your face,
when I wake in the morning,
Smiles at me in the dawn's rosy light.

****

All alone tonight I wait
Down beside the garden gate,
Where I waited for you oft in days of yore;
When the music of your voice
Always made my heart rejoice,]
As you came to meet me from the cottage door.
I was happy all day long,
Ere Death hushed love's old sweet song,
Even yet, I hear its echo soft and low,
When the evening stars shine out
They pierce through the clouds of doubt,
And I'll hear the song again, sometime, I know.

I TRIED ANYWAY

Teacher thinks that I'm a poet,
Could be so . . . but I don't know it,
Still, I'll have to try my hand,
Or in Dutch I'm sure to land.
Some folks write swell cowboy stories,
Some of lands of ancient glories,
Some of love and some of war,
Some of sun and moon and star,
Some of that and some of this,
Books that end in one big kiss;
Some write of adventure's trail,
Some tell tales to turn you pale;
Seems 'most everyone can write,
I'll just try my luck tonight.
Not a lone idea will come,
I just sit here feeling dumb,
Guess I'll have to take a zero,
Wish I was a movie hero,
Then I'd write myself a check,
Go and spend it too, by heck,
I'd sure cut a fancy caper.
Gee! I've used up all my paper

BIG BUTCH, LITTLE BUTCH

By Mae Poloson

I sat today at my grandson's table,
And I looked at all the silverware they'd placed
around my plate;
And tryin' to behave as well as I was able,
I was so darn busy that I don't know what I ate.
I smiled as I thought of how times are changin',
I laughed as I remembered, then, the way we used to eat.
We had no silver with its smart, precise arrangin',
Knives and forks to go around was counted quite a treat.
It was Big Butch, Little Butch, Old Case, and Cob Handle,
Help yourself to one of them
While I hunt up a candle.
The way the vittles vanished,
It surely was a scandal,
When we started in with
Big Butch, Little Butch, Old Case and Cob Handle.
This here new way of eatin'
Has got a feller guessin',
Are we all just havin' dinner
Or is this a jugglin' lesson?
When it comes to carvin' vittles
This new stuff can't hold a candle
To big Butch, Little Butch,
Old Case and Cob Handle.

My mind knows this may not be true,
And your mind knows it too;
But the heart of me will always know,
That the story here, is true.

For the mind must have the proof of things,
Clear as the stars above,
The heart surveys the evidence,
Through the mystic lens of love.

SPRING TIME

Do you remember Springtime long ago,
Side by side, we watched the bright river flow;
I said, "I love you, do love me too?"
Softly you answered me, "Yes, dear, I do."

Later you told me you'd made a mistake,
Then you were gone, and I felt my heart break.
Spring will return with its flower-sprinkled hills,
Blue skies and songbirds, and soft murmuring rills.

But to my heart, springtime cannot return,
Lonely I'm waiting and always I yearn
For the lost happiness that we once knew;
Why cannot hearts, like the springtime be true?

Star of the Western woodland,
Light of the forest glade,
Turn your light upon me,
Pretty Indian maid.

Shine upon my pathway,
Always when I roam,
Star of the Western forest,
Guide me safely home.

Star of the Western forest,
Ever shine for me,
Pretty Indian maiden,
Light my dark teepee.

WAITING FOR A LETTER

One year ago I left you, dear, and said a fond farewell'
How sad that parting made me feel, no tongue or pen can tell
Your letters cheered me for a while, but now they come no more
Still my sad heart cannot believe that love's sweet dream is o'er.
I wait and hope anew each day, a message sweet from you
Will come to drive my doubt away and tell me you're still true.
Waiting for a letter, long, long overdue,
Watching every morning 'til the mail comes through.
Every day I wait
By the old front gate,
Waiting for a letter, saying you are true.

DON'T' THINK YOU'RE THE WHOLE CORN FIELD

My Ma warned me all about you,
But I laughed at all her fears,
She said you'd only break my heart,
And fill my eyes with tears.
And now you come to say goodbye,
You've proved that she was right,
Don't' stick around to watch me cry,
I'll cry alone, tonight.
But when my heart has mended, and
I'm older, wiser too,
I'll find myself another man,
A better man than you.
And I'll forget my broken heart,
You'll cause me no more tears,
For you're not the whole corn-field
Just because you've got two big ears.

Don't think you're the whole corn-field,
Just because you've got two big ears;
I'm going to find me a better man,
As soon as I dry my tears.
I'm going to laugh at my broken heart,
In happier, future years;
Don't think you're the whole corn-field,
Just because you've got two big ears.

WHEN GOLDEN AUTUMN LEAVES ARE DRIFTING DOWN

I am thinking of a quiet little valley far away,
Where the sheltering hills are decked with Autumn's gold,
I remember how I left there, just a year ago today,
With a smile that hid a weight of grief untold.
But my long exile is over and I'll soon be going home,
To a winsome little maid with eyes of brown;
And the sadness and the waiting we'll forget them as we roam
Where the golden Autumn leaves are drifting down.
Where the golden Autumn leaves are drifting down,
Waits a winsome little maid with eyes of brown,
And those eyes with love did shine as she promised to be mine
Where the golden Autumn leaves were drifting down.

Odds & Ends

The magpie makes a grating sound,
Like scraping half-burnt toast,
And yet of all the birds around
He's the one who talks the most.

False teeth are a penalty
We pay for growing older,
And a berry seed beneath them
Seems bigger than a boulder!

In days of old when knights were bold,
And fought for ladies fair,
A knight could prove undying love
In battles here and there.
But time speeds on, now comes the dawn
Of other days and fashions,
A man today need only say,
"Please darling, share my rations."

Tuffy

Ghost of a little white mongrel dog,
Why do you follow me?
Can you not stay in the shadow-land
Where your canine soul is free?

Little white dog with the brave, true eyes,
I buried your body deep,
Then hurried back to my daily tasks
 For you would not have me weep.

But still I can hear your padding feet
And your softly panting breath,
For your loyal soul is slow to yield
To the sudden hand of death.

Little white ghost, go sleep in peace,
For you were a loyal friend,
Here's to the hope we shall meet again,
Out where the dim trails end.

Starlight, Star Bright

Far in the West a lone, bright star
Scatters its gold on the purple peaks,
And as I look on its light afar,
Softly the voice of memory speaks,
Speaks of a lonely little maid,
Facing the West at the close of day,
Half believing and half afraid,
Memory speaks, and I hear her say"

"Star light, Star bright,
First star I see tonight,
I wish I may, I wish I might
Have the wish I wish tonight."

Could I turn back the clock of time,
Knowing life's road would be steep and rough,
I would repeat the old, old rhyme,
Making one wish, 'twould be enough.
I would wish for a sheltering roof,
A little money and one true friend,
Holding these things to be ample proof,
Life is worth living until the end.

UNFINISHED ECHOES

Echoes from childhood's sweet laughter,
Echoes from Love's golden dawn,
Sound in the heart ever after,
Long after Youth's dreams are gone.

Why do I keep this worn old chair?
Its' wobbly and out of style,
But I can remember when you sat there,
And looked at me with a smile.

I do not like to say "Goodbye",
Not even to a foe.
I felt we might be loyal friends,
But now, I'll never know.

(I Believe)

Some believe that the dead return,
To the ones they left behind,
I believe that they never go,
But the proof I hard to find.

I believe, in some mystic realm,
That the soul and mind of me
Will live and look on a world at peace
In the better days to be.

To a Sparrow

Noisy fellow, I am goind,
Soon no more I'll hear or see
All your rowdy congregation
In the seedling apple tree.

You'll not miss me in the Summer,
Scarcely know that I am gone,
But I wonder who will feed you
In the stormy winte dawn?

When the snow falls, I'll remember
How you watched the kitchen door,
How you grabbed the food I threw you
And then loudly ordered more.

Your're a greedy little heathen,
And you voice is far from sweet,
But you're welcome, little sparrow,
To the many crumbs you eat.

For altho they say a greater
Pest than you is seldom found,
You're the only one who keeps me
Company the year around.

I will not weep alone and say
"My golden dream is o'er".
For it was mine one happy day,
Tho now it comes no more.

It brightened all the dreary years
With many a rainbow gleam,
And I must not blot out, with tears,
The memory of my dream.

Come back Elaine

My dear, do you know that, a long time ago
I built me a castle in Spain?
Brightly it gleams in my garden of dreams,
Waiting for you, my Elaine
But love waits in vain in my castle, Elaine,
His light from the window shines out,
'Tis seeking for you but cannot pierce through
The shadows of sorrow and doubt.

Chorus:
Come back, Elaine, to my castle in Spain,
Come where Love's beacon light gleams
Sadly I wait, here at the gate,
That leads to my garden of dreams.
Come to my heart, and no more depart,
Leaving me lonely, Elaine;
Dreams will come true, dear one, when you
Come back to my castle in Spain.

The garden, Elaine, of my castle in Spain,
Now shelters a bleeding heart,
Fanned by the breeze, the dark cypress trees
Sigh as the song-birds depart.
The carrier dove, with its message of love,
Is winging to you, my Elaine,
To bid you return where love's fires burn,
Here in my castle in Spain.

Envy

I built me a shelter, snug and dry,
'and laughed at the stormy weather,
But laugher died when two passed by,
Facing the storm together.

Shadows

Darkly the shadows fall,
From the old trees so tall,
And from the moss—grown wall, Darkly and sadly.
Now hiding from my view,
Paths gemmed with evening dew,
Where oft I walked with you,
Joyously, gladly.

Deep in the heart of you,
Lived there a love so true,
And from your eyes shown through,
How could I doubt you?
How could I doubt your love,
Think you would faithless prove, Dooming me here to rove,
Sadly without you?

Could you come back to me,
Then from all doubting free,
I'd ever truthful be,
Trustful and tender.
Then would love's bright star shine,
Then would its rays diving
Flood all your way and mine,
With their soft splendor.

I am dreaming tonight just one more hopeless dream,
And as usual I'm dreaming of you.
But of sunshine or hope there is never a gleam,
Just a dream that can never come true.

Now I have reached the object of my homing,
I'd not exchange foe Islands of the Blest.
My restless feet can cease their aimless roaming,
My weary heart can fold its wings and rest.

CHRISTMAS EVE IN RATTLESNAKE GULCH

It's the night before Christmas, not even a mouse
Will deign to be caught in the old ranch house.
And so with no tom-cats their movements to hamper,
Away they all go, with a hop, skip and scamper.

The family too, feels the urge to cut capers,
I hope that their antics don't get in the papers,
Fred's off at a party by a guy named George Wells,
And Pa's set on raising assorted mild hells.

And Bert goes along to bring Pa back alive,
I hope they roll in not later than five!
And daughter's gone too, with her eyes all alight,
As she thinks of the friends she'll be meeting tonight.

And I sit here wondering if Tippy can keep
The roving coyotes from stealing the sheep.
For the sheep are alone, and I'll bet a button
Each sly roving raider is dreaming of mutton.

And Tippy's so small, the poor little sinner,
He'd just about serve to garnish their dinner.
The sheep are alone, and it seems rather hard,
For one little dog, all alone, to stand guard

On a few thousand dollars that's still on the hoof,
Camped on a hillside, the sky for a roof.
St. Nick, if you're passing, and keeping a log,
Just enter this item: "one little black dog,

Just one little dog and an old crippled dame,
Were guarding the ranch when Christmas Morn came."

Broken Toys

And so you have come back to me,
And say you love me yet,
The empty years, the broken vows,
You ask me to forget.
You ask me to believe again
New promises you'd make.
Why don't you ask me to forget
How hearts feel when they break?

You broke my toys in childhood days,
And seemed to think it smart.
You haven't greatly changed since then,
Now you prefer a heart
You held it in your careless hands,
Its love you freely take,
And then you cast the heart aside,
And smile to see it break.

You broke my toys in childhood days,
And I forgave you then,
But I have changed, if you have not,
I can't forgive again.

I might have bought another toy
To ease my young heart-ache,
But I have only one poor heart,
The one you chose to break.

Where the cottonwoods are whisp'ring to the breeze,
O'er my little old grey cabin 'neath the trees,
O'er the prairies' well-known track,
Someday I'll be going back
Tho 'I've traveled far on alien land an seas.

Where the cottonwoods are whisp'ring to the breeze,
O'er my little old grey cabin 'neath the trees,
There my loved ones wait for me,
And someday with them I'll be,
Where the cottonwood are whisp'ring to the breeze.

Where the cotton woods are whisp'ring'
By a cool and bubbling spring,
And the lone coyote's singing
Was a melancholy ring.
There a sun-bleached cabin nestles
Close beside the whisp'ring trees

Once when my days work was over,
It was there I took my ease,
There's a well-worn path a-winding
To the old nail-studded door.
There's a dear one cooking supper,
While a child plays on the floor.

I have seen fair palm fringed islands
Ringed about with silver foam,
But to me they're not so lovely
As my prairie cabin home.

Just Because I Love You

Why do my thoughts ever stray to you, dear,
Why am I lonely when you're not here,
Why do I wish you were always near?
Because, dear heart, I love you.

Chorus:
Just because I love you,
That is why, dear heart,
I'll be ever faithful
Ne'er from you I'll part.
Just because I love you,
That's the reason, dear,
I would keep you near me,
Always, always near.

Promise me, dear, that you will be true,
Faithful to me as I am to you,
I want you near me, life's journey through,
Because, dear heart, I love you.

BRIEF RETURN

dreamed of a paw raked down the door,
And I said, "It's Barney, come home once more."
I opened the door at his urgent whine,
And said, "come in, little dog of mine."
With joyous motion he leaped inside,
Straight to my arms that were open wide,
And then both the dog and the dream were gone,
I knew, as I waited the lonely dawn
Barney had died as the moon sank low,
But in my heart I'll always know
A loyal fried made a gallant try
And help death off while he said goodbye.

My mind knows this may not be true,
And your mind knows it too,
But the heart of me will always know
That the story here, is true.
For the mind must have the proof of things,
Clear as the stars above,
But the heart surveys the evidence'
Thru the mystic lens of love.

Blue Eyes From Texas

I thought I'd go to the rodeo,
Folks told me it was quite a show . . .
I had some doubt, but I went out,
And when I got there I looked about,
And then Oh me! Oh my!
I saw a slight that took my eye . . .
A tall cowboy came strolling along,
Whistling the tune of an old-time song;
I stepped in his way, he tipped his hat,
I looked in his eyes and that was that.

Blue eyes from Texas, they stole my heart,
Blue eyes from Texas, they have the art
Of looking at you with their bright deep blue
With a glance that is straight and brave and true.
Blue eyes from Texas, blue as the sea,
Blue eyes from Texas, smiling at me,
Blue eyes from Texas, I dream of them yet,
Blue eyes from Texas, I cannot forget.

I never knew that I would miss you
So very much, but now you're gone.
I hear your voice in all my dreaming,
I see your face in each new dawn.

If you would just return to me, dear,
I ask no better gift of fate,
Than just to hold you close and love you,
I wonder if I've learned, too late.

That all my dreams are built around you
That all my hopes of joy to be

Will die unless I know, beloved,
That someday you'll come back to me.
At least I know how much I love you,
I know my heart is yours alone.
For all the pain I may have caused you,
Awakened love awaits to atone.

If I were teaching history,
Its wars, its age-old hates,
I'd try to tell the why of it,
And never mind the dates.

For men have died by thousands,
And thousands still must die,
While history emphasizes when,
But seldom tells us why.

You, teachers in your classrooms,
Put by your outworn slates,
And do not feed youth's hungry minds
A mass of useless dates.

But help them find the reasons
For our tumultuous world,
Then war's dark blood-stained banners
Some day may all be furled.

Where the bees are softly humming
In the garden where we met,

I am waiting for your coming,
For my heart cannot forget.
Tho' I live for memory only,
Still my heart cannot regret
Tho 'walk forever lonely,
In the garden where we met.

Tho' I walk forever lonely
In the garden where we met,
I am glad I loved you only,
And my heart cannot forget.

Each Heart Knoweth Its Own Bitterness

Well Parson, you've read from the sacred book,
And you've handled your subject well,
But what can you know, in this sheltered nook
Of a place that you call Hell?
For Hell's not a place; it's a state of mind,
And each man fashions his own,
Then hides the key where none can find,
And lives in his Hell alone.
In my own hell, old memories sprout,
Like a poisonous, choking vine,
And the only fruit they bear is doubt,
Which makes a bitter wine.
There is doubt of self and doubt of friend,
And doubt of a God above,
But the bitterest doubt in all the blend
Is doubt of a woman's love.
But still I live in my hell of doubt,
I made it, the fault is mine,
Myself shut in, my friends shut out,
I drink my bitter wine.

He was a roving bandit,
From town to town he rambled,
The cash he'd always land it,
In places where he gambled.

For if he could not win it,
He'd just hold up the place,
Take all the money in it,
His six-gun was his ace.

This bad man's special pleasure
Was robbing safes and banks,
He'd loot them of their treasure,
Than smile and murmur, "Thanks".

One day he dropt in Cheyenne,
And shot a cashier down,
The cops were hot as cayenne,
And chased him from the town.

The bandit started running,
But started just too late.
Those cops, they started gunning,
Death was the bandit's fate.

They buried him near the city,
No minister or coffin,
They said, "it in a pity
We can't do this more often."

His sweetheart saw him buried,
The sad tears she was shedding.
She said, "We can't be married,
That dumb cop spoiled the wedding."

She whispered, Goodbye honey",
And left his lonely grave.
But stopped to get his money,
And smooth her finger wave.

She said, "It's him I'm loving,
But he's wiped off the map,
So now, I must be moving
To find another sap."

Grace E Larson

Her eyes were full of tear-drops,
And gosh, she did look cute,
She shook her diamond ear-drops,
And said, "I'm off to Butte."

And so she left him lonely,
Beneath a Russian thistle,
No sound disturbs him, only
A freight train's lonely whistle.

So, pause awhile and ponder,
If you think crime will pay,
The lad that's sleeping yonder
Thought just the same one day.

God of the Nation

God of the Nations,
Hear our prayers
And bid oppression cease.
Let right triumphant vanquish might,
And victory bring peace.

Grant that our valiant ones who died
May not have died in vain.
Let Freedom be a monument
Above the brave ones slain.

Dive Death from all the land and sky,
And from the farthest sea,
Let people build their homes again,
Secure, serene and free.

Yes, once again, let peace descend
O'er all the war-torn work,
And grant, O God, that freedom's flag
May ne'er again be furled

Odds and Ends

The purple sage, so Zane Grey found
Was fine for men to ride thru,
But now it is so finely ground
We'd smother if we tried to.

Tears and beer (to' 'Old Fritz

As I wandered down town yester even'
And stopped at my favorite café,
There I saw a lone stranger just grievin'
And drinking his whole life away.
I said, "May I sit here beside you'
And list' to your sad tale of woe,
Will you tell me what evils betide you
That dim all of life's rosy glow?"

He answered, "Kind sir, I'm your debtor,
Your kindness my sad heart does cheer,
I've just had bad news in this letter,
I'm drowning my sorrow in beer.
And if you would care to sit down here,
I'll give you the letter, "he said,
"Then you'll know what sorrow I drown here."
And these are the words that I read:

I'll forgive all your amorous glances,
At the cuties you meet on your way.
I'll forget that you always take chances
With the cash that you get on pay-day.
You may step on my favorite bunion,
And I'll cherish you still in my heart,
But you won't give up garlic and onion,
So I'm sorry to say, we must part.

There's a place where the rose-buds are swelling,
On a cute little island I know,
And it's there I'll establish my dwelling,
Where the onion and garlic won't grow."

Grace E Larson

I finished the sorrowful message,
And wiped at a sad, falling tear,
And then thro' the evening's slow passage
We both sat and cried in our beer.

HONEY CHILE

Honey Chile, Honey Chile,
You've been gone for quite awhile,
How I've missed your sunny smile,
Honey Chile, Honey Chile.
Honey Chile, my heat would break,
If you should decide to take
All your smiles to some far isle,
Honey Chile, Honey Chile.
I'll be lonely all the while,
Nothing could my heart beguile,
If I lost your sunny smile,
Honey Chile, Honey Chile.
Honey Chile, don't go away,
Promise me that you will stay,
That we two no more will part,
That you'll always warm my heart,
With you smile, Honey Chile.

"Sure That's Different"

If one goes 'round just talking
To himself, they say "he's nuts,
Yes, positively crazy."
And one hasn't got the guts
To thus offer his neighbors
With his harmless little chatter
He isn't brave enough to say
"It really doesn't matter,"
But one can take the idle words
And write them in a poem,
And all his neighbors smile at him
And boast how well they know 'im,
And yet the thoughts expressed may still
Be just as dim and hazy
A little printing draws the line
On being sane or crazy.

This habit of conversing
With oneself, one has to fight it,
So stop that mumbling to yourself,
Be sane, sit down and write it!

I thought I'd write a thought each day
And then thought "Maybe not",
For I must say, one thought a day
Is one more than I've got.
And so if I should write today,
Some other's thoughts I'd borrow,
It seems to me, 'twould fairer be
To wait and write tomorrow.

Now you're just a memory buried deep within my heart,
Once you were the world to me, and we vowed we'd never part.
Tho' you're just a memory as I wander sad and lone,
And your face no more I'll see, in my heart, you're still my own.

Splash

By Mae Poloson

She made disparaging remarks
About his helicopter,
Just as they flew above the lake,
So that was why he dropter.

False Teeth are a punishment
We take for growing older,
And a berry seed beneath them
Seems bigger than a boulder.

I used to plan what I would do when rationing was over,
When I'd have meat for me to eat and bones to toss to Rover.
But rationing is over now, it is an outworn fashion,
So now I sigh for times gone by, when there was meat to ration.

Valentine

My pillow is wet while I think of you, dear,
And this fact, I think, should be proof,
Of how much I miss you; I wish you were here,
To fix that darned leak in the roof.

DREAMS

I will not mourn its passing now, altho the dream is o'er,
For it was mine one happy day, but it will come no more.
It brightened many a dreary hour, with all its rainbow gleam,
God, let me close my eyes in death, Ere I forget to dream.
And dying, may I will my dreams to Youth, to dream once more,
For all good things were once but dreams, to someone gone before.

IF I HAD WINGS

!
If I had wings with which to fly,
To all the lands beneath the sky,
I'd fly and try To find the why
Of many things.
If I had wings,
But plodding feet the long day through,
Are nearer to the little thing,
The tender things,
That I would miss,
If I had wings

I live in a place called Rattlesnake Gulch
Where we use snake skins for garden mulch
It's rattlesnakes here and it's rattlers there,
The blame things really get in my hair.
It's snakes in the pantry and under the bed,
A sheepherder once found a snake in his bread.
Then he went to the stove to kindle a fire,
He woke a rattler and he roused its ire,
It was under the stove, and it moved, you bet,
It moved so fast that the stove upset.
The coffee and beans flew far and wide,
And the poor old herder sat down and cried.
But the old-timer says, "It ain't so bad,
You oughta seen the snakes when I was a lad,
They were so darn thick, so help me, Pete,
A feller didn't dare set down his feet.
There were so many snakes not a flower could bloom,
And all they had was standin' room.
And When a snake traveled, he walked on his tail,
If this ain't so, may I rot in jail!"

Beloved

I love you, dear, I love you so,
My heart would die, if you should go.
Your are the sunshine in my skies,
You kindle love lights in my eyes.
You are the center of my world,
Your bright hair 'round my heart is curled.
My heaven in your eyes I see,
Your hands hold life's best gifts to me.
Once more I say, I love you so,
My heart would die if you should go.

HICKORY WHISTLE

Down o'er the vale from the hill above,
Softly as down from thistle
Comes now a message from one I love
Played on a hickory whistle.
High on the hill waits a brown-eyed boy,
Calling me there to meet him
While my young hear beats time with joy,
Gladly I haste to greet him.

Oft in the twilight here I wait,
Just for the whistle's calling,
And as I lean on the old front gate,
Softly its notes are falling,
Poets may sing of the carrier dove,
With its sweet message winging,
Sweeter to me is the note of love,
Heard in the whistle's singing.
Once more it floats o'er the vale below,
Lightly as down from thistle,
Swiftly my feet o'er the daisies go,
I'm coming, hickory whistle.

There's a light across the valley
And its clear and steady gleam
Makes me think of my dear Hallie,
Makes me pause awhile and dream.
For that light across the valley
Is a beacon light of home,
And my thoughts around it rally
Tho' from it, I have to roam.

There's a light across the valley,
And it's shining just for me,
It was placed there by my Hallie,
And it's waiting she will be,
There's a light across the valley,
And it bids me not to dally,
But to hasten home to Hallie,
Who is watching now, for me.

MOONSTRUCK

If you didn't mean it,
We will blame it on the moon,
But if you really love me,
Call me up at noon.

Don't' tell me that you love me,
When the moon is shining bright,
I'll believe anything
On a moonlight night.

But oh, the next day,
The magic fades away,
Romance is out,
I'm full of doubt,

And oh so very blue.
I hate to grieve you,
I'd like to believe you,
Was it just the moon,
Would you say the same at noon
If the month were gray
November And not dreamy, luscious June?
Darling, tell me true,
For I'm asking you,
But don't just say you love me
When we're looking at the moon,
If you really mean it, call me up at noon.
The Nth Freedom

I have come back to the quiet hills,
Far from the noise of the riotous crowds,
Here with the songs of the birds and the rills,

Here where the tall trees are kissing the clouds.
Here I can drink from a cool crystal spring,
Here I can rest on a flower-sprinkled knoll,
Lulled by the song that the little winds sing,
Here I find peace for both body and soul.
Here I find surcease from fretting and care,
And . . . yes, one more item I'm adding to these . . .
Free of the crowd with its cold, hostile stare,
I can eat garlic whenever I please!

COYOTE

Night is waiting, pale and still,
For the stars to light the sky,
From the timbered slope of the towering hill
Comes an eerie and mournful cry,

Coyote, want does it mean, this cry
That you send on the waiting air?
Each time I hear I, I wonder why
It tells of a soul's despair.

Even your laughter, free and wild,
That sounds from the canyon deep,
Is but the laugh of a frightened child,
Who laughs, for he dare not weep.

Coyote, you with your Devil's ears,
And your slyly mocking face,
How can you voice all the griefs and fears
That trouble the human race?

Oft, as you travel the hidden trail,
Where your countless kind have trod,
I hear at night your mournful wail,
Like a soul in search of god.

Coyote, what is this God you seek,
Scarcely hoping to find?
Does He dwell on a mountain peak,
 And is he cruel or kind?

All these things I wish I knew,
Vainly my groping mind
Seeks for the answer just as you
Seek what you cannot find.

Restless, seeking, we both must go
On to the lonely end,
Meeting only as foe meets foe,
Never as friend meets friend.

But someday if you pass a mound,
Where I lie beneath the dos,
Pause, for my soul may be hovering 'round,
And we'll both go in search of God.

Indian Summer Waltz

Faintly a melody floats on the breeze,
Thru' the dark cedars the lights softly glow,
Bringing to mind all the sweet ecstasies
Love brought to us just one short year ago.
Promising happiness, whispering love,
Dreamy and soft came the stains of the waltz,
Seeming as true as the heavens above,
Who could believe that its message was false?

indian Summer Waltz
Indian Summer Waltz
How our melody yet stirs my heartstrings,
Indian Summer Waltz
Was you message false,
Must our love bring naught but tears and partings?
Indian Summer Waltz
With its promise false,
Once it seemed a tune from fairy finger,
Indian Summer Waltz
Indian Summer Waltz
Always in my heart the echo lingers.

Song of the Unknown Road

If you can sing when your heart is breaking,
If you can smile when your hope is gone,
Then come with me o'er the way I'm taking,
Though clouds obscure the coming down.

For though the clouds are all dark and lowering,
And none may know what lies ahead,
The searching soul though the darkness souring,
Brings back new hopes for old ones dead.

Then come with me o'er the road I'm taking,
Just take my hand and journey on,
For in the east is the pale light breaking,
And hand in hand we'll greet the dawn.

I remember a cute little pup,
With a fierce little "Bow wow wow",
 But the cute little pup, he had to grow up,
And nobody wants him now.
Florida, the Land of Flowers

Long ago when I was younger,
And I thought myself so wise,
I developed quite a hunger
 Just to roam 'neath foreign skies.
So I said goodbye to Mother,
Dad and all my friends at home,
And I fondly kissed another,
As she begged me not to roam.

Now I get a lonely feeling,
As I view the scenery grand,

And a little wish comes stealing
Just to be in my own land.
Where m y sweetheart waits to greet me
'Neath the sunny, perfumed bowers,
With a kiss I know she'll meet me,
When I reach that land of flowers.

Florida, the Land of Flowers,
I am coming back to you,
And beneath the perfumed bowers,
I shall greet my sweetheart true.
For she's waiting for my coming,
Dreaming of love's gladsome hours,
While my airplane's swiftly humming
Onward, to the Land of Flowers.

RIDING THRU THE SILVER SAGE WITH YOU

Dear, tonight I'm weary, longing for the prairie,
Waiting for the happy time when I'll return to you;
Desolate and lonely, I am wishing only
Just to smell the silver sage as we go riding through.
Riding through the silver sage with you,
Neath a Summer sky of baby blue,
Where the cooing dove, softly calls it's love,
Just as my heart calls, dear one, to you.

Days creep slowly by, but the time draws night
When my fondest dreams will all come true,
When again I'll be on the prairie free,
Riding thru the silver sage with you.

THE LITTLE BLACK DOG

The little tan dog had a little black pup,
And his eyes were bright as buttons.
And I said, "little dog, you are much too fine
To chase the roving muttons."

The little black pup was a special pup,
And really I'm not spoofing,
For the little black pup said, "Bip, bip, bip!"
While the other pups were woofing.

The little black dog grew swift and strong
As he raced o'er hill and hollow,
A rider climbed to the highest point,
And the little black dog would follow.

But the little black dog would never scorn
A path both safe and lowly'
He liked to take long walks with me,
Though I could walk but slowly.

Sometimes we'd walk across the field
And watch the sunset fading,
Or, when the sun at noon was hot,
I'd take the black dog wading.

The little black dog was a happy dog,
And his bark was bright and cheery,
But he cried sometimes in the moonlit night,
Like a soul with earth cares weary.

The other dogs howled and I went outside,
To try to stop the riot.
The little black dog sang a pagan prayer,
I listened, and was quiet.

One night he sang to his pagan god,
And I think he did it, knowing
Before the next full moon was high,
To new fields he'd be going.

The little black dog went out one day,
Down the trail of no returning.
I must learn to take my walks alone,
But it's slow and weary learning.

SHINING STAR

Down beside a bright and sparkling river,
Flowing from the snow-clad hills afar,
Where the leafy branches gently quiver,
Sleeps an Indian maid called Shining Star.
Years ago a young Chief loved this maiden,
Treasures of the hunt to her he'd bring.

Oft as he returned with trophies laden,
To his Shining Star he'd softly sing:

My Shining Star, light of my life you are.
Guide me with your rays so true.
My Shining Star, oh guide me from afar,
Till I reach my home and you."

But as hand in hand their way they wended,
Jealous eyes were watching from afar,
And an arrow, for the chief intended,
Pierced the loved heart of Shining Star.
Many years have passed since they were together
Wandered where the river flows along.
Yet the famous Chieftain Eagle Feather,
By a lonely grave, oft sings this song:

My Shining Star, light of my life you are.
Guide me with your rays so true.
My Shining Star, oh guide me from afar,
Till I reach my home and you."

Homesick

Oh, the wind blows free on the Western plain,
And its whisper reaches me,
And it seems to say, "Come back again,
Where the range is broad and free."

There's a little house on the Western plain,
With its logs bleached silvery white,
And a light shines out through its window pane,
To guide me through the night.

There's a girl who waits on the Western plain,
And her eyes are truest blue,
She said, "When you return again,
I'll be waiting here for you."

So I'm off today on the fastest train,
To the girl who waits for me,
And we'll settle there on the Western plain,
Where the range is wide and free.

TREES AND WATER

Trees and water,
Water and trees;
How I have hungered
And thirsted for these.
Trees to sit under,
Water to splash in,
Water for small, shining
Fishes to flash in.
Trees and water,
Water and trees;
God, let me never
Stray far from these.

Signs of Spring

The poets sing of birds in Spring,
And silver streams and lakes;
Could they but stand on this dry land,
They'd sing of rattlesnakes.

Beanery Babe's Busted Romance

I saw the letter once again
And saw my hand was shaking;
I stopped and stared at nothing, then,
 And knew my heart was breaking.

The people in the dining room
Were chattering like parrots,
As I began once more to groom
The onions, spuds and carrots.

And through the deadly ache there rose
A gleam of humor stealing,
No broken heart should come to those
Who spend their lived in peeling

The unromantic cousin of
The fair and fragile lily;
I sad "I will not die for love,
And weeping would be silly."

And those beside me never knew
My heart was slowly dying;
One said, "When I peel onions too
It always sets me crying."

First Rattler

I found a rattlesnake today,
My mom she came and killed it.
She had a pail of chicken feed,
But hurried, so she spilled it.

That big ol' snake was all coiled up,
His rattles just a-buzzin'.
You shoulda heard the noise he made,
It sounded like a dozen.

But Mom, she grabbed the garden hoe
And swatted that ol' rattler.
When my mom starts to kill a snake,
She surely is some battler!

Sometimes she hits it just one time,
But mostly she hits twenty.
But you can bet, when she gets through,
That ol' snake's had a-plenty.

I'd like to wear 'em in my hat
Like once my Uncle Tom did,
So folks would think I killed the snake,
Unless I told them Mom did1

I've lived for more than thirty years
Since all my world seemed ended.
My broken heart now brings no tears,
For Time, the break has mended.
But when I see some fresh, young face,
With love and dreams all glowing,
I feel a little pang that says,
"Old girl, your heart is showing."

To Rattlesnake from Rattlebrain

You're different from the bullsnakes,
And one difference is this:
You make a fearful rattling
While the bullsnakes only hiss.

And the bullsnake's no more dangerous
Than a biting dog or cat,
But when you bite us and we die,
You can just say, "Well, that's that."

And you and I are different,
I don't know just all the ways,
But I'm sure that we'll be different
'Til we end our earthly days.

You wear your rattles on your tail,
While mine are in my head;
But we'll share the earth together
As the unimportant dead.

RIDING UP TO GRAPEVINE HOLLOW

Riding up the trail with you,
Nicest thing a guy could do,
Listening to your happy song,
As our ponies jog along.
Gee, kid, this is just the life,
How'd you like to be my wife?
Here's a ring if you'll just wear it,
I'll be good to you, I swear it.
I'll be true as stars above you,
What I means, kid, is, I love you.

Riding up thro' Grapevine Hollow,
Lead the way, sweetheart, I'll follow.
When we reach the highest peak,
Where the warm winds kiss your cheek,
Darling, I'll feel mighty blue,
If I cannot kiss you too.
Why can't we team up for live?
You'd sure make me one swell wife.
Then we'd ride Life's trail straight thro',
You for me, and me for you.

BLACK DUCK

Black Duck, Black Duck, walking sedately,
I have found traces of enemies lately;
Yapping on the rocky hill, tracks in the loam,
Black Duck, Black Duck, stray not from home.
Poor friendly Black Duck, useless my warning,
Stealthy steps tracked her, one foggy morning.
Black Duck is gone; now, in sun or rain,
I walk alone, going after grain.
Black Duck is missing, vanished altogether,
 Farewell message, one black feather.

There grows a plant upon this hill
That's tall and stately when it's still,
But when the winds its seed cups shake,
It sounds quite like a rattlesnake.
Once I believed in early youth,
That Nature holds the key to truth.
But where find truth beneath the sky,
When even a pale, dead plant can lie?

GRAY WOLF'S DANCE

They came to the reservation and asked if I would go
And do the dance my people did so many moons ago.
They peeped in all our teepees and they praised our scenery grand,
Next day they took the iron trail that leads to movie land.

And I, Gray Wolf, went there with them, for I alone did know
The customs of my people here so many moons ago.

Hoo yah, hoo yah, hoo yah hoo,
I've been to movie land,
It's all colossal grand,
How they live thru the things they do
I'll never understand.

AT first the strange new sights and sounds were all my heart desire
But then I soon lost interest and of them I quickly tired.
For I could see in my mind's eye an old smoke-stained teepee,
And knew a slender dark-eyed girl was waiting there for me.
And if I cannot soon behold that teepee by the lake,

I fear I'll find with some surprise, that Indian hearts can break.

Hoo yah, hoo yah, hoo yah hoo,
Before the moon shall wane,
I'll take the fastest train,
And when I see my own teepee
I'll never stray again.

RURAL ROMANCE

Out where the wild plover
Sings low to its mate,
A sad, rustic lover
Leans over a gate.
A song he is singing
To someone unseen,
While bright birds are winging
Their way o'er the green.
I paused there to hear him,
And so did the birds,
And, being quite near him,
We both heard these words:

Tillie, my Tillie meet me by the corn,
Oh, come to your Willie when you hear the cowhorn.
I'll be waiting, Tillie, right here by the barn;
Come, walk with your Willie, out under the stars.
If you fail me, Tillie, I'll be so forlorn,
Oh, come to your Willie, when you hear the cow horn.

LITTLE NEW HOUSE

Little new house with your waiting air,
Little new house with your rooms all glowing,
You are just wasted on me. I care
Not for the charms you insist on showing.
Little new house, there is no new bride,
For she's dead, tho' she stands her talking,
Robbed of her faith, her hope and her pride,
What you see is a zombie walking,
Little new house, I shall not stay here,
Soon I shall go to a cottage older,
For you were made for a young bride's cheer,
Not for a good h eart, still growing colder.
 Little new house, I shall say goodbye,
Leave you for someone with joy a-beaming,
Tell her to look in the cupboard high,
There I have left her my hopes and dreaming.

Circumstantial Evidence

A Holstein calf, intent on fun
Was galloping o'er the sod;
 His Holstein sire, on a rocky knoll,
Was posed like a heathen God.

The calf grew tired of playing alone,
As he circled the grassy field,
And he said, "I'll challenge that calf out there,
And we'll see which one shall yield."

And so he galloped across the field,
And then he stopped with a jolt;
For what he thought was a Holstein calf
Was really a pinto colt.

The calf looked long at the pinto colt,
(That calf was a cynical lad),
Then scratched his head on a nearby post,
And turned and looked at his dad,

And what he was thinking, no one knows,
A fellow could only guess;
For the colt was spotted just like the bull,
And men have been hanged for less!

LEGEND OF THE WAR DRAGON

In a mountain cave in a country fair
A fiery dragon slept,
And when it woke and left its lair
The people mourned and wept.

For when it crept from its fiery cave
And wandered the earth again,
Each track it left was a giant grave
Where they buried a thousand men.

And the people feared it would come again,
Tho quiet for years and years,
For it loves to drink of the blood of men
That's flavored with women's tears.

But the old ones said there was once a sword
That could pierce the dragon's heart,
On its blade engraved was a magic word
That could bid their fears depart.

And they asked, "Is there one among us all
Who can find this sacred blade
That will free our land from the dragon's thrall
And the havoc it has made?"

And one there was among the throng
Who kissed his love farewell,
And he said, "I go, tho the road be long
Tho it lead thru the gates of Hell".

And he traveled fast and he traveled west
And he searched the world around,
And he tarried not for love nor rest,
'Til the magic blade was found.

But the wonder sword was sheathed in rust
And the word was almost gone,
Still he said as he wiped away the dust
"I will take the trail at dawn".

So he tracked the dragon to its lair
Its crimes he could not forgive,
He drew his sword and he slew it there,
That the sons of men might live.

But the people feel its fiery breath
As they pass by its loathsome cave,
For its soul comes forth on the feet of death
And measures men for the grave.

And tho it is dead, it may live again
Tho it sleeps for a thousand years,
It may drink once more of the blood of men
That is flavored with women's tears.

So cherish ye well, the sacred sword
To guard it, ye sons of men,
Lest tarnish fall on the magic word
 And the dragon walk again.

EPILOGUE

The Sacajawea Hotel and Three Forks in 2014, 104 years after Mae Poloson got off the train nearby at logan, MT. Logan remains with a few scattered homes. Three Forks is thriving with close to 2000 in population. Tourism is a big draw with excellent fishing and beautiful scenery. The Missouri River begins very near Three Forks where the Gallatin, Jefferson, and Madison Rivers come together.!

The Sacajawea Hotel offers 29 luxurious guest rooms with spa inspired bathrooms. Guests can enjoy fine dining, a bar, and live music. The hotel is classified as Historical with few changes in decor inside or outside.

Just to think that Grandma Mae walked on and cleaned the same floors I have walked on several times; the last was in 2010 when I started this family history.

The land where Grandma Mae homesteaded near Three Forks is now in wheat. The Wheat Montana Bakery is nearby.!

The Poloson Ranch was sold just before Dan Poloson's death. It had 2 different owners then was sold to the Flathead tribe. The last time I went to see the ranch the house was a shambles and it had been one of the nicest homes in the area. Windows and light fixtures broken, cupboards missing, upstairs bathroom fixtures lie broken, and apparently the basement had about 8000 lbs of garbage grew about.!

When Mom and Fred had gone to see the place Fred commented that giving it back to the rattlesnakes was a good idea.

The hard work and dreams of An Immigrant, A Homesteader, And Sheep are alive in family memories even though there's very little evidence the ranch had existed as a busy, happy place. Kids and grandkids, the bleat of several thousand sheep, the bawling of cattle, and the neigh of the horses as well as the beautiful views, the orchards, and that smell of sage; all are in the past but my hope is that this book will record my family's history for generations to come.

www.ingramcontent.com/pod-product-compliance
Ingram Content Group UK Ltd.
Pitfield, Milton Keynes, MK11 3LW, UK
UKHW022229230426
12048UKWH00016BA/1140